THE ULTIMATE BOXING QUIZ BOOK

THE ULTIMATE BOXING QUIZ BOOK

Compiled by Ralph Oates
Foreword by Barry J. Hugman

APEX PUBLISHING LTD

First published in hardback in 2009 by
Apex Publishing Ltd
PO Box 7086, Clacton on Sea, Essex, CO15 5WN, England
www.apexpublishing.co.uk

Copyright © 2009 by Ralph Oates
The author has asserted his moral rights

British Library Cataloguing-in-Publication Data
A catalogue record for this book
is available from the British Library

ISBN: 1-906358-64-8   978-1-906358-64-8

All rights reserved. This book is sold subject to the condition, that no part of this book is to be reproduced, in any shape or form. Or by way of trade, stored in a retrieval system or transmitted in any form or by any means, electronic, mechanical, photocopying, recording, be lent, re-sold, hired out or otherwise circulated in any form of binding or cover other than that in which it is published and without a similar condition, including this condition being imposed on the subsequent purchaser, without prior permission of the copyright holder.

Typeset in 10.5pt Chianti Bdlt Win95BT
Cover Design: Siobhan Smith
Cover photograph of Ricky Hatton: Les Clark

Printed in Great Britain by the
MPG Books Group, Bodmin and King's Lynn

ACKNOWLEDGMENTS:
I would like to thank Ruby Oates and Howard Oates for their assistance in checking the facts in this book.

Please note: Every effort has been made to ensure that the information contained within this book is correct. However the author and the publisher do not accept any liability for any loss sustained due to the use of information in this book.

FOREWORD

There can be no doubt that when you think about boxing quiz books the name Ralph Oates springs to mind. Ralph has, through sheer hard work, become recognised as the leading compiler of boxing quiz books in the country. To have published World Heavyweight Boxing Champions Elite (1987) Know Your Boxing (1991) Boxing Clever (1994) Boxing Shadows (1997) The Heavyweight Boxing Quiz Book (2002) The Muhammad Ali Boxing Quiz Book (2007) and now The Ultimate Boxing Quiz Book is most certainly proof that he stands alone in his chosen field. Ralph, a former junior amateur boxer, has an enthusiasm for the sport that only those who have participated in it could understand. With his diligence and eye for detail, just like the other books he has compiled The Ultimate Boxing Quiz Book is sure to be a success. His expertise on the subject also made him an obvious choice to write a column for the Essex Courier, which ran for almost three years. Ralph also produces articles and quizzes for my British Boxing Board of Control Boxing Yearbook, and in so doing it is noticeable that his knowledge on the subject matter enables him to interview fighters from both the past and present with a clear understanding of what makes them tick, as only someone that has been in the ring himself can do. I am certain that The Ultimate Boxing Quiz Book will prove to be another best-seller for Ralph, and his well-researched facts will make you think long and hard about the events that have taken place in the ring over the years. I thoroughly recommend The Ultimate Boxing Quiz Book to all fans of the sport.

Best wishes
Barry J. Hugman
Editor and compiler of The British Boxing Board of Control Boxing Yearbook

INTRODUCTION

Boxing is a sport that over the years has produced many exciting moments and with it an equal number of memories that we can often call upon from time to time when talking about our favourite fights or boxers in general. Now and again, however, a fact can slip our minds or we find that our recollections of specific details of events have faded with the passing of time, so for instance we might recall a contest that we are sure had ended with a points decision, whereas it had actually finished when the referee stopped the bout. This, I feel, is what makes a quiz book on your favourite sport an interesting challenge. Clearly many fans of the game will be able to answer certain questions fairly easily and quickly, but others might have followers of the noble art thinking long and hard and then resorting to searching for any relevant record books to find the definitive answer. It would be true to say that it is very difficult these days to specify who is really the actual world champion in any respective weight division, as various governing bodies duly recognise a different world title holder at any one time. So it is therefore refreshing and good for the game that more often than not the rival champions at the same weight do eventually meet in the ring to do battle and thus determine who is the better man. The sport has its critics, of that there is no doubt, but nevertheless boxing has produced a number of great fighters who are known the world over, even by non-followers of the game - men such as Joe Louis, Muhammad Ali, Rocky Marciano, Sugar Ray Robinson, Lennox Lewis and many, many more, who have been a credit both inside and outside of the ring. I hope you will enjoy the many questions in this book and indeed have fun finding out just how much you know about that square ring and those who perform inside the ropes.

Best wishes
Ralph Oates

www.apexpublishing.co.uk

ROUND 1
THE PRIZE-FIGHTING DAYS - 1

Go back in time and answer the mixed bag of questions about the fighters who fought during the bare-knuckle period

1. In which year was Daniel Mendoza born – 1763, 1764 or 1765?

2. Ben Caunt was listed as how tall - 6 foot 2.5 inches, 6 foot 4 inches or 6 foot 5 inches?

3. What was the nickname of James Burke - The Deaf 'Un, The Silent 'Un or The Strong 'Un?

4. What was the nationality of Tom Molineaux – British, French or American?

5. Which fighter was known as The Napoleon of the Prize Ring - Tom King, Tom Sayers or Aaron Jones?

6. Over how many rounds did Jem Mace outpoint opponent Bill Thorpe on 17 February 1857 – 18, 19 or 20?

7. True or false: Jem Mace was nicknamed The Gypsy?

8. Where in England was John Gully born – Bristol, Manchester or Liverpool?

9. True or false: John Gully spent a period of time in debtors prison?

10. Which fighter was known as The Benicia Boy - John Camel Heenan, Tom Johnson or George Meggs?

ROUND 2
THE PRIZE-FIGHTING DAYS - 2

11. During his time James Figg set up an amphitheatre where he instructed sports and staged contests. Where was the amphitheatre located – Manchester, London or Liverpool?

12. Which fighter was known as The Tipton Slasher - Harry Sellers, Jack Slack or William Perry?

13. What was the real name of Tom Spring - Thomas Winter, Thomas Summer or Thomas Springton?

14. In which year was Tom Cannon born – 1788, 1789 or 1790?

15. What was the nickname of Tom Cannon - The Great Gun of Windsor, The Great Gun of London or The Great Gun of Manchester?

16. In which year was John L. Sullivan born – 1858, 1859 or 1860?

17. What does the 'L' stand for in John L. Sullivan – Lionel, Lewis or Lawrence?

18. What was John L. Sullivan's nickname - The Strong One, The Man of Iron or The Boston Strong Boy?

19. John L. Sullivan was listed as how tall - 5 foot 10.5 inches, 5 foot 11 inches or 6 foot?

20. On 10 March 1888 John L. Sullivan defended his bare-knuckle world heavyweight title against challenger Charley Mitchell. What was the result - Sullivan won by a knockout in round 8, Mitchell won by a stoppage in round 12 or It was declared a draw after 39 rounds?

ROUND 3
WHAT'S MY FIGHTING NAME? - 1

Which name did the following boxers adopt when embarking on a fighting career?

21. Thomas Rocco Barbella (former world middleweight champion) - Rocky Graziano, Jake La Motta or Carl (Bobo) Olson?

22. Giuseppe Antonio Berardinelli (former world light-heavyweight champion) - Gus Lesnevich, Anton Christoforidis or Joey Maxim?

23. William J. Breslin (former world welterweight champion) - Jack Britton, Mike Glover or Pete Latzo?

24. Judah Bergman (former world light-welterweight champion) - Mushy Callahan, Jack (Kid) Berg or Johnny Jadick?

25. Arnold Raymond Cream (former world heavyweight champion) - Ezzard Charles, Joe Louis or Jersey Joe Walcott?

26. Rafelle Capabianca Giordano (former world welterweight champion) - Young Corbett III, Tommy Freeman or Jimmy McLarnin?

27. Gerardo González (former world welterweight champion) - Marty Servo, Kid Gavilan or Fritzie Zivic?

28. Francisco Guilledo (former world flyweight champion) - Pancho Villa, Fidel LaBarba or Albert Frenchy Belanger?

29. Johnny Gutenko (former world bantamweight champion) - Pete Herman, Joe Lynch or Kid Williams?

30. Joseph Francis Hagen (former world light-heavyweight champion) - Philadelphia Jack O'Brien, Jack Dillon or George Gardner?

ROUND 4
WHAT'S MY FIGHTING NAME? - 2

31. Richard Ihetu (former world middleweight and light-heavyweight champion) - Eddie Cotton, José Torres or Dick Tiger?

32. Samuel Lazzaro (former world welterweight champion) - Joe Dundee, Young Jack Thompson or Jackie Fields?

33. Joseph Robert Loscalzo (former world flyweight champion) - Victor Young Pérez, Midget Wolgast or Willie La Morte?

34. Rocco Francis Marchegiano (former world heavyweight champion) - Jack Dempsey, Gene Tunney or Rocky Marciano?

35. Gershon Mendeloff (former world welterweight champion) - Mike Glover, Barney Ross or Ted (Kid) Lewis?

36. Guglielmo Papaleo (former world featherweight champion) - Willie Pep, Jackie Wilson or Albert (Chalky) Wright?

37. Louis Phal (former world light-heavyweight champion) - Battling Levinsky, Battling Siki or Paul Berlenbach?

38. Walker Smith Jr (former world welterweight and middleweight champion) -Terry Downes, Sugar Ray Robinson or Emile Griffith?

39. Carmine Orlando Tilelli (former world middleweight champion) - Joey Giardello, Carmen Basilio or Gene Fullmer?

40. Anthony Florian Zaleski (former world middleweight champion) - Billy Soose, Tony Zale or Ken Overlin?

ROUND 5
NUMBER OF PROFESSIONAL BOUTS - 1

How many professional bouts did the following boxers have during their career (all of whom won a world title in their respective weight division)?

41. Frank Bruno – 43, 44 or 45?

42. Ezzard Charles – 121, 122 or 123?

43. John Conteh – 39, 40 or 41?

44. Terry Downes – 43, 44 or 45?

45. Joe Frazier – 35, 36 or 37?

46. Rocky Graziano – 82, 83 or 84?

47. Paul Hodkinson – 24, 25 or 26?

48. Maurice Hope – 34, 35 or 36?

49. Paul Ingle – 23, 24 or 25?

50. Duke McKenzie – 46, 47 or 48?

ROUND 6
NUMBER OF PROFESSIONAL BOUTS - 2

51. Charlie Magri – 33, 34 or 35?

52. Rocky Marciano – 48, 49 or 50?

53. Terry Marsh – 26, 27 or 28?

54. Alan Minter – 47, 48 or 49?

55. Floyd Patterson – 63, 64 or 65?

56. Sugar Ray Robinson – 199, 200 or 201?

57. Luis Rodríguez – 120, 121 or 122?

58. John H. Stracey – 51, 52 or 53?

59. Jim Watt – 45, 46 or 47?

60. Howard Winstone – 67, 68 or 69?

ROUND 7
FIRST DEFEAT - 1

Who were the first boxers to defeat the following in the professional ranks (all of whom held a world title in their respective division during their career)?

61. Terry Allen (flyweight) - Jackie Bryce, Alex Murphy or Rinty Monaghan?

62. Sammy Angott (lightweight) - Lee Sheppard, Leonard Del Genio or Johnny Hutchinson?

63. Tommy Burns (heavyweight) - Mike Schreck, Philadelphia Jack O'Brien or Jack (Twin) Sullivan?

64. Eugène Criqui (featherweight) - Lucien Vinez, Robert Dastillon or Jack Gatehouse?

65. Johnny Famechon (featherweight) - Max Murphy, Gilberto Biondi or Ray Spackman?

66. Bob Foster (light-heavyweight) - Doug Jones, Mauro Mina or Allen Thomas?

67. Frankie Genaro (flyweight) - Howard Mayberry, Bushy Graham or Harry Leonard?

68. Rocky Graziano (middleweight) - Joe Agosta, Charley Ferguson or Steve Riggio?

69. Don Jordan (welterweight) - Dickie Wong, Andy Escobar or Art Aragon?

70. Gus Lesnevich (light-heavyweight) - Jackie Aldare, John Anderson or Frankie Caris?

ROUND 8
FIRST DEFEAT - 2

71. Joe Louis (heavyweight) - Ezzard Charles, Rocky Marciano or Max Schmeling?

72. Sandro Mazzinghi (light-middleweight) - Giampaolo Melis, Nino Benvenuti or Charley Austin?

73. Freddie Mills (light-heavyweight) - George Davis, Eddie Gill or Jack Lewis?

74. Rinty Monaghan (flyweight) - Paddy Ryan, Jim Keery or Jackie Paterson?

75. José Nápoles (welterweight) - Hilton Smith, Tony Pérez or Alfredo Urbina?

76. Carl (Bobo) Olson (middleweight) - George Duke, Boy Brooks or Dave Sands?

77. Sugar Ray Robinson (welterweight and middleweight) - Jake LaMotta, Randy Turpin or Ralph (Tiger) Jones?

78. Lionel Rose (bantamweight) - Ray Pérez, Singtong Por Tor or Fernando Sotelo?

79. Randy Turpin (middleweight) - Albert Finch, Jean Stock or Gordon Wallace?

80. Albert (Chalky) Wright (featherweight) - Joey Valarde, Ray Davis or Joe Hernandez?3

ROUND 9
YEAR OF BIRTH - 1

In which year were the following boxers born (all of whom won a world title during their professional careers)?

81. Muhammad Ali (heavyweight) – 1940, 1941 or 1942?

82. Ken Buchanan (lightweight) – 1944, 1945 or 1946?

83. John Conteh (light-heavyweight) – 1951, 1952 or 1953?

84. Michael Dokes (heavyweight) – 1958, 1959 or 1960?

85. Joe Frazier (heavyweight) – 1943, 1944 or 1945?

86. Maurice Hope (light-middleweight) – 1949, 1950 or 1951?

87. Don Jordan (welterweight) – 1933, 1934 or 1935?

88. Joe Louis (heavyweight) – 1914, 1915 or 1916?

89. Benny Lynch (flyweight) – 1912, 1913 or 1914?

90. Freddie Mills (light-heavyweight) – 1917, 1918 or 1919?

ROUND 10
YEAR OF BIRTH - 2

91. Alan Minter (middleweight) – 1950, 1951 or 1952?

92. Carlos Monzón (middleweight) – 1940, 1941 or 1942?

93. Floyd Patterson (heavyweight) – 1935, 1936 or 1937?

94. Sandy Saddler (featherweight and super-feather weight) – 1924, 1925 or 1926?

95. John H. Stracey (welterweight) – 1949, 1950 or 1951?

96. Mike Tyson (heavyweight) – 1965, 1966 or 1967?

97. Rodrigo Valdéz (middleweight) – 1946, 1947 or 1948?

98. Jim Watt (lightweight) – 1946, 1947 or 1948?

99. Howard Winstone (featherweight) – 1938, 1939 or 1940?

100. Tony Zale (middleweight) – 1911, 1912 or 1913?

ROUND 11
DID NOT MEET - 1

Which opponent did the following boxers not meet in the professional ranks?

101. Muhammad Ali - Jerry Quarry, Oscar Bonavena or Scott LeDoux?

102. Frank Bruno - Joe Bugner, Herbie Hide or Bill Sharkey?

103. Ken Buchanan - Victor Paul, Tommy Tiger or Al Keen?

104. John Conteh - Larry Sykes, Johnny Frankham or Fred Lewis?

105. Hugo Corro - Rodolfo Rosales, Emile Griffith or Willie Warren?

106. Roberto Duran - Jimmy Batten, Saoul Mamby or Jim Watt?

107. Chris Eubank - Herol Graham, Les Wisniewski or Anthony Logan?

108. Joe Frazier - Ray Staples, Don Waldhelm or Charley Polite?

109. Maurice Hope - Dave Adkins, Len Gibbs or Mickey Flynn?

110. Sugar Ray Leonard - Marvin Hagler, Aaron Pryor or Thomas Hearns?

ROUND 12
DID NOT MEET - 2

111. Joe Louis - Lee Epperson, Lee Ramage or Lee Savold?

112. Charlie Magri - Mike Stuart, Bryn Griffiths or Charlie Brown?

113. Joey Maxim - Hubert Hood, Tom Reddington or Lou Brooks?

114. Alan Minter - Bobby Watts, Tony Licata or Trevor Francis?

115. Ken Norton - Wayne Kindred, Julius Garcia or Rodell Dupree?

116. Vicente Saldivar - Dwight Hawkins, Richie Sue or Alberto Soto?

117. John H. Stracey - Henry Rhiney, Willie Rea or Dante Pelaez?

118. Arnold Taylor - Evan Armstrong, Luis Aisa or Shigeyoshi Ohki?

119. Jim Watt - Perico Fernandez, Jimmy Revie or Pedro Carrasco?

120. Carlos Zarate - Jorge Torres, Johnny Clark or Juan Ordóñez?

ROUND 13.
THE FIRST ROUND - 1

How many times did the following world champions win a contest in the first round during their professional careers?

121. Virgil Akins (welterweight) – 1, 2 or 3?

122. Muhammad Ali (heavyweight) – 1, 2 or 3?

123. Terry Allen (flyweight) – 3, 4 or 5?

124. Nigel Benn (WBO middleweight and WBC super-middleweight) - 11, 12 or 13?

125. Frank Bruno (WBC heavyweight) – 12, 13 or 14?

126. Marcel Cerdan (middleweight) – 13, 14 or 15?

127. John Conteh (WBC light-heavyweight) – 4, 5 or 6?

128. Joe Frazier (heavyweight) – 4, 5 or 6?

129. Rocky Graziano (middleweight) – 9, 10 or 11?

130. Masahiko (Fighting) Harada (flyweight and bantamweight) – 1, 2 or 3?

ROUND 14.
THE FIRST ROUND - 2

131. Lennox Lewis (heavyweight) – 5, 6 or 7?

132. Rocky Marciano (heavyweight) – 10, 11 or 12?

133. Salvador (Dado) Marino (flyweight) – 4, 5 or 6?

134. Freddie Mills (light-heavyweight) – 13, 14 or 15?

135. Rinty Monaghan (flyweight) – 3, 4 or 5?

136. Floyd Patterson (heavyweight) – 1, 2 or 3?

137. Vicente Saldivar (featherweight) – 1, 2 or 3?

138. José Torres (light-heavyweight) – 1, 2 or 3?

139. Randy Turpin (middleweight) – 7, 8 or 9?

140. Jim Watt (WBC lightweight) – 1, 2 or 3?

ROUND 15
FIRST PROFESSIONAL
OPPONENT - 1

Whom did the following boxers meet in their first professional contest?

141. Muhammad Ali - Herb Siler, Tony Esperti or Tunney Hunsaker?

142. Cornelius Boza - Edwards - Tommy Wright, Paul Clemit or Barry Price?

143. Frank Bruno - Rudi Gauwe, Lupe Guerra or Ron Gibbs?

144. Johnny Caldwell - Moncef Fehri, Michel Lamora or Billy Downer?

145. John Conteh - Tony Burwell, Okacha Boubekeur or Frank Bullard?

146. Jimmy Ellis - Arley Seifer, Rory Calhoun or Wilf Greaves?

147. Johnny Famechon - Salvatore Casabene, Sammy Lang or Nick Wells?

148. Bob Foster - Ernie Knox, Duke Williams or Floyd McCoy?

149. Prince Naseem Hamed - Des Gargano, Shaun Norman or Ricky Beard?

150. Lloyd Honeyghan - Dai Davies, Alan Cooper or Mike Sullivan?

ROUND 16
FIRST PROFESSIONAL OPPONENT – 2

151. Maurice Hope - Len Gibbs, John Smith or Pat Brogan?

152. Lennox Lewis - Al Malcolm, Bruce Johnson or Noel Quarless?

153. Dave (Boy) McAuley - Dave Smith, John Mwaimu or Roy Williams?

154. Barry McGuigan - Selvin Bell, Terry Pizzaro or Gary Lucas?

155. Charlie Magri - Bryn Griffiths, Nessim Zebilini or Neil McLaughlin?

156. Johnny Nelson - Magne Havnaa, Doug Young or Peter Brown?

157. Floyd Patterson - Sammy Walker, Eddie Godbold or Lester Jackson?

158. Robin Reid - Julian Eavis, Andrew Furlong or Mark Dawson?

159. Lionel Rose - Mario Magriss, Jackie Bruce or Billy Brown?

160. Mike Tyson - Trent Singleton, Hector Mercedes or Don Halpin?

ROUND 17
FIRST PROFESSIONAL OPPONENT - 3

Whom did the following boxers meet in their first professional contest?

161. Arthur Abraham - Frank Kary, Petr Rykala or Sladko Cizicz?

162. Joe Calzaghe - Stinger Mason, Paul Hanlon or Spencer Alton?

163. Miguel Cotto - Jason Doucet, Jacob Godinez or Waklimi Young?

164. Ricky Hatton - Robert Álvarez, Kid McAuley or David Thompson?

165. David Haye - Saber Zairi, Roger Bowden or Tony Booth?

166. Bernard Hopkins - Clinton Mitchell, Keith Gray or Ed Tyler?

167. Zab Judah - Pablo Tejeda, Michael Johnson or José Torres?

168. Mikkel Kessler - Alex Lubo, Michael Corleone or Kelly Mays?

169. Jeff Lacy - Jerald Lowe, Tommy Attardo or Tony Pope?

170. Enzo Maccarinelli - Paul Bonson, Mark Williams or Nigel Rafferty?

ROUND 18
FIRST PROFESSIONAL OPPONENT - 4

171. Floyd Mayweather Jr - Reggie Sanders, Jerry Cooper or Robert Apodaca?

172. Manny Pacquiao - Rocky Palma, Pinoy Montejo or Ting Ignacio?

173. Gavin Rees - Graham McGrath, Ernie Smith or John Farrell?

174. Antonio Tarver - Tracey Barrios, Jason Burrell or Joaquin Garcia?

175. Jermain Taylor - Chris Walsh, Kenny Stubbs or Antonio Baker?

176. James Toney - Ronnie Yoe, Stephen Lee or Carl Penn?

177. Nikolai Valuev - Alex Vassilev, John Morton or Alexey Tzigankov?

178. Junior Witter - John Green, Cam Raeside or Lee Molyneux?

179. Clinton Woods - Paul Clarkson, Earl Ling or Dave Proctor?

180. Ronald (Winky) Wright - Anthony Salerno, Christopher Conrad orTony Graham?

ROUND 19
NOT IN THAT COUNTRY - 1

In which country did the following former world champions NOT box during their professional careers?

181. Muhammad Ali (heavyweight) – England, Denmark or Germany?

182. Terry Allen (flyweight) – Italy, Egypt or Spain?

183. Nino Benvenuti (WBA light-middleweight and middleweight) – America, Germany or England?

184. Ken Buchanan (lightweight) – Mexico, America or Japan?

185. John Conteh (WBC light-heavyweight) – America, Denmark or Germany?

186. Joe Frazier (heavyweight) – England, Australia or Japan?

187. Susumu Hanagata (WBA flyweight) – England, America or Thailand?

188. Maurice Hope (WBC light-middleweight) – America, Italy or Canada?

189. Ismael Laguna (lightweight) – Argentina, France or Germany?

190. Charlie Magri (WBC flyweight) – America, Italy or Spain?

ROUND 20
NOT IN THAT COUNTRY - 2

191. Alan Minter (middleweight) – America, Spain or Italy?

192. Carlos Monzón (middleweight) – England, America or Italy?

193. José Nápoles (welterweight) – Canada, France or Germany?

194. Floyd Patterson (heavyweight) – Sweden, England or France?

195. Eusebio Pedroza (WBA featherweight) – Japan, Belgium or England?

196. Lionel Rose (bantamweight) – America, England or Japan?

197. John H. Stracey (WBC welterweight) – America, Italy or Mexico?

198. Franco Udella (WBC light-flyweight) – England, Switzerland or Australia?

199. Jim Watt (WBC lightweight) - South Africa, America or Spain?

200. Howard Winstone (WBC featherweight) – Mexico, Italy or America?

ROUND 21
NATIONALITY - 1

What is the nationality of the following fighters (all of whom have held a world title during their respective careers)?

201. Henry Armstrong – English, American or French?

202. Mbulelo Botile - South African, Australian or Russian?

203. Frank Bruno – American, Canadian or English?

204. Tommy Burns – Canadian, American or Australian?

205. Josue Camacho - Puerto Rican, Mexican or South African?

206. Harold Dade – Mexican, French or American?

207. Gustavo Espadas – Spanish, Mexican or Argentinian?

208. Pedro Flores – Panamanian, Spanish or Mexican?

209. Marvin Hagler - Canadian, American or Columbian?

210. Takenori Hatakeyama – Venezuelan, Japanese or Puerto Rican?

ROUND 22
NATIONALITY - 2

211. István Kovács – Hungarian, Russian or Italian?
212. Peter Kane – American, Australian or English?
213. Rafael Limón - Puerto Rican, Mexican or American?
214. Sandro Lopopolo – Spanish, Italian or American?
215. Benny Lynch – Scottish, Australian or Canadian?
216. Manuel Medina – American, Mexican or Puerto Rican?
217. Pinkey Mitchell – American, Canadian or English?
218. Mike Tyson – Canadian, American or South African?
219. Howard Winstone – Welsh, Scottish or Irish?
220. Pernell Whitaker – Mexican, Cuban or American?

ROUND 23
WHICH WEIGHT? - 1

In which weight division did the following boxers hold a professional world title?

221. Lou Ambers – Bantamweight, Featherweight or Lightweight?

222. Hogan (Kid) Bassey – Flyweight, Bantamweight or Featherweight?

223. Curtis Cokes – Lightweight, Welterweight or Middleweight?

224. Tiger Flowers – Lightweight, Welterweight or Middleweight?

225. Al Hostak – Welterweight, Middleweight or Light-heavyweight?

226. Hilmer Kenty – Lightweight, Welterweight or Middleweight?

227. Pone Kingpetch – Flyweight, Bantamweight or Featherweight?

228. Ted (Kid) Lewis – Lightweight, Welterweight or Middleweight?

229. Mike McTigue – Middleweight, Light-heavyweight or Heavyweight?

230. Bob Montgomery - Bantamweight, Featherweight or Lightweight?

ROUND 24
WHICH WEIGHT? - 2

231. Davey Moore – Bantamweight, Featherweight or Lightweight?

232. Claude Noel – Lightweight, Welterweight or Middleweight?

233. Carl (Bobo) Olson – Lightweight, Welterweight or Middleweight?

234. Rafael Ortega – Bantamweight, Featherweight or Lightweight?

235. Manuel Ortiz – Bantamweight, Featherweight or Lightweight?

236. Johnny Saxton – Featherweight, Lightweight or Welterweight?

237. Battling Siki – Welterweight, Middleweight or Light-heavyweight?

238. Billy Soose - Middleweight, Light-heavyweight or Heavyweight?

239. Marcel Thil – Welterweight, Middleweight or Light-heavyweight?

240. Chalky Wright – Flyweight, Bantamweight or Featherweight?

ROUND 25
NAME THE REFEREE - 1

What is the first name of the following referees?

241. Adams – Ben, Tim or Paul?

242. Cavalieri – Nino, Luis or Guido?

243. Davies – Richie, Jimmy or Alan?

244. De Wiele - Anton Van, Daniel Van or Carlos Van?

245. Foster – Bobby, Steve or Howard?

246. Green – Mark, Phillip or Ben?

247. Habighorst – Alberto, Timo or Rafael?

248. Hinds – Colin, Jeff or Frank?

249. John-Lewis – Ricky, Carl or Ian?

250. Jones – Wynford, Dai or Steven?

ROUND 26
NAME THE REFEREE - 2

251. Loughlin – Sammy, Richard or Victor?

252. Meronen – Erkki, Curt or Nikolai?

253. O'Connor – Steve, Casey or Terry?

254. Parris – Dave, Chris or Benny?

255. Spampool – Athanus, Thabo or Agnaldo?

256. Steele – Denny, Calvin or Richard?

257. Thomas – Paul, Ken or Brian?

258. Vann – Martin, Mickey or Dennis?

259. Verbeke – Mikael, Rikard or Philippe?

260. Weeks – Johnny, Tony or David?

ROUND 27
TRUE OR FALSE? - 1

Which of the following statements are true and which are false?

261. Freddie Miller won the world featherweight title during his professional career.

262. Former world lightweight champion Benny Leonard was born in 1893.

263. Former world flyweight champion Fidel LaBarba won a gold medal in the 1924 Olympic Games at flyweight.

264. Former world bantamweight champion Pete Herman had 149 contests during his professional career.

265. Heavyweight title challenger Tommy Gibbons was born in 1895.

266. Former world middleweight, heavyweight and light-heavyweight champion Bob Fitzsimmons boxed in the southpaw stance.

267. Jack Dillon won the world middleweight title during his professional career.

268. Former world light-heavyweight champion Maxie Rosenbloom was nicknamed Slapsie Maxie.

269. Former world bantamweight champion Kid Williams was born in Denmark.

270. Former European champion Karl Mildenberger was the first boxer with the southpaw stance to challenge for the world heavyweight title.

ROUND 28
TRUE OR FALSE? - 2

271. During his professional career British and Commonwealth flyweight champion John McCluskey challenged once for the world championship.

272. During his professional career former WBC world, European and British lightweight champion Jim Watt did not box in Mexico.

273. Former European, British and Commonwealth heavy weight champion Henry Cooper once held a version of the world heavyweight title.

274. Howard Winstone, the former WBC world, European and British featherweight champion, won a gold medal at featherweight in the Commonwealth Games (then Empire) in 1958.

275. During his professional career former British and Commonwealth middleweight champion Johnny Pritchett won a Lonsdale belt outright.

276. During his professional career former world, European and British middleweight champion Alan Minter boxed twice in Denmark.

277. European and British heavyweight title contender Billy Walker was nicknamed The Blond Bomber.

278. Frank Bruno, the former WBC world and European champion, was born in 1964.

279. Markus Beyer held the WBC world super-middleweight title during his professional career.

280. Heavyweight contender Billy Walker fought twice in America during his career.

ROUND 29
NAME THE SOUTHPAW – 1

Can you name the only fighter in each question, from the past to the present, who boxed in the southpaw stance?

281. Tim Austin, Ismael Laguna or José Legrá?

282. Frank Bruno, Bob Foster or Cornelius Boza-Edwards?

283. Ricky Hatton, Joe Calzaghe or Larry Holmes?

284. Terry Downes, Keith Holmes or Ken Buchanan?

285. Tiger Flowers, Walter McGowan or Henry Akinwande?

286. Marvin Hagler, Roy Jones Jr or Shannon Briggs?

287. David Haye, Michael Moorer or Felix Sturm?

288. Ruslan Chagaev, Carl Froch or Jhonny González?

289. Steve Molitor, Jermain Taylor or Ricardo Torres?

290. Krzysztof Wlodarczyk, Zab Judah or Sam Peter?

ROUND 30
NAME THE SOUTHPAW - 2

291. Lennox Lewis, Pongsaklek Wonjongkam or Mzonke Fana?

292. Alan Minter, Carlos Monzón or John H. Stracey?

293. Shane (Sugar) Mosley, Stipe Drews or Kermit Cintron?

294. Miguel Cotto, Celestino Caballero or Herbie Hide?

295. In-Jin Chi, Ivan Calderon or Javier Castillejo?

296. Manny Pacquiao, Gairy St Clair or Nobuo Nashiro?

297. Antonio Tarver, Silvio Branco or Wladimir Klitschko?

298. Howard Winstone, Joan Guzmán or Robert Guerrero?

299. Oleg Maskaev, James Toney or Jim Watt?

300. Mikkel Kessler, Juan Urango or Brian Viloria?

ROUND 31
WHO'S THAT LADY? - 1

The next section is dedicated to the women that over the years have contributed greatly to boxing in various ways, be it as boxers, managers, promoters, etc. Can you identify them?

301. Who was the first female in Britain to be given a professional boxing licence by The British Boxing Board of Control - Cathy Brown, Jane Couch or Michelle Sutcliffe?
302. Who was the first woman to be appointed as a judge in America - Carol Polis, Eugenia Williams or Carol Castellano?
303. Who was the first female Administrative Steward for the British Boxing Board of Control - Tania Follett, Judith Rollestone or Alma Ingle?
304. What is the nickname of American female boxer Christy Martin - The Coal Miner's Daughter, The Fire Chief's Daughter or The Police Chief's Daughter?
305. Who was the first British female MC - Charlotte Russell, Lisa Budd or Judith Rollestone?
306. Who was the first female judge to officiated at a world heavyweight title fight - Debra Barnes, Eugenia Williams or Eva Shain?
307. Who became the second British female MC - Charlotte Russell, Lisa Budd or Annette Conroy?
308. When in defence of his WBA world heavyweight title Riddick Bowe stopped challenger Jesse Ferguson in 2 rounds on 22 May 1993, this was the first time that three female judges had officiated - Eugenia Williams, Shelia Harmon-Martin and who else - Carol Castellano, Patricia Jarman or Eva Shain?
309. Who was the first female second in British Boxing - Tania Follett, Annette Conroy or Christine Rushton?
310. Katherine Morrison was the first female promoter from which country – Wales, Ireland or Scotland?

ROUND 32
WHO'S THAT LADY? - 2

311. Which female boxer was nicknamed The Fleetwood Assassin - Cathy Brown, Jane Couch or Juliette Winter?

312. What is the nationality of female boxer Regina Halmich – French, Spanish or German?

313. Who became the first British female to be licensed as a boxing manager - Judith Rollestone, Tania Follett or Charlotte Russell?

314. True or false: American boxer Lalia Ali is the daughter of former three-times world heavyweight champion Muhammad Ali?

315. Which female boxer was nicknamed The Bitch - Cathy Brown, Juliette Winter or Shanee Martin?

316. When Wladimir Klitschko retained his WBO world heavyweight title by stopping challenger and former holder of the crown Ray Mercer in round 6 on 29 June 2002 in Atlantic City, this was the first time that a woman had promoted a world heavyweight title fight. Who was she - Jackie Kallen, Diane Lee Fischer or Carol Polis?

317. Who became the first female promoter in the north-east of England - Annette Conroy, Alma Ingle or Christine Rushton?

318. True or false: when Laila Ali retained her WBC and WIBA super-middleweight world titles on 3 February 2007 by stopping challenger Gwendolyn O'Neil in round 1, this was the first professional female boxing contest to be staged in South Africa?

319. Which of the following ladies boxes in the southpaw stance - Holly Holm, Cathy Brown or Jane Couch?

320. Which female boxer received an MBE in 2007 - Cathy Brown, Shanee Martin or Jane Couch?

ROUND 33
BRITISH CHAMPION IN WHICH WEIGHT DIVISION? - 1

In which weight division did the following boxers hold a British title?

321. Brian Anderson – Welterweight, Light-middleweight or Middleweight?

322. Jimmy Batten – Welterweight, Light-middleweight or Middleweight?

323. Mickey Cantwell – Flyweight, Bantamweight or Featherweight?

324. Maurice Core – Middleweight, Light-heavyweight or Heavyweight?

325. Hughroy Currie – Middleweight, Light-heavyweight or Heavyweight?

326. John Doherty – Featherweight, Super-featherweight or Lightweight?

327. Gordon Ferris – Middleweight, Light-heavyweight or Heavyweight?

328. Ali Forbes – Middleweight, Super-middleweight or Light-middleweight?

329. Tommy Glencross – Flyweight, Bantamweight or Featherweight?

330. Frank Grant – Welterweight, Middleweight or Light-heavyweight?

ROUND 34
BRITISH CHAMPION IN WHICH WEIGHT DIVISION? - 2

331. Joey Jacobs – Bantamweight, Featherweight or Super-featherweight?

332. Tee Jay - Light-heavyweight, Cruiserweight or Heavyweight?

333. Joe Kelly – Flyweight, Bantamweight or Featherweight?

334. Davy Larmour – Bantamweight, Featherweight or Super-featherweight?

335. Kevin Lueshing – Welterweight, Light-middleweight or Middleweight?

336. Des Morrison – Lightweight, Light-welterweight or Middleweight?

337. Alan Richardson – Bantamweight, Featherweight or Lightweight?

338. Terry Spinks – Flyweight, Bantamweight or Featherweight?

339. Wally Swift Jr – Welterweight, Light-middleweight or Middleweight?

340. Tony Willis – Lightweight, Light-welterweight or Welterweight?

ROUND 35
DOUBLE BRITISH CHAMPIONS - 1

In which weight division did the following boxers NOT hold a British title?

341. Dennis Andries – Middleweight, Light-heavyweight or Cruiserweight?

342. Johnny Basham – Welterweight, Middleweight or Light-heavyweight?

343. Joe Bowker – Bantamweight, Featherweight or Lightweight?

344. Don Cockell – Middleweight, Light-heavyweight or Heavyweight?

345. Pat Cowdell – Featherweight, Super-featherweight or Lightweight?

346. Johnny Cuthbert – Featherweight, Lightweight or Welterweight?

347. Joe Fox – Flyweight, Bantamweight or Featherweight?

348. Herol Graham - Light-middleweight, Middleweight or Light-heavyweight?

349. Bunny Johnson – Middleweight, Light-heavyweight or Heavyweight?

350. Tancy Lee – Flyweight, Bantamweight or Featherweight?

ROUND 36
DOUBLE BRITISH CHAMPIONS - 2

351. Jock McAvoy – *Welterweight, Middleweight or Light-heavyweight?*

352. Walter McGowan – *Flyweight, Bantamweight or Featherweight?*

353. Dave Needham – *Flyweight, Bantamweight or Featherweight?*

354. Jackie Paterson – *Flyweight, Bantamweight or Featherweight?*

355. Jack Petersen – *Middleweight, Light-heavyweight or Heavyweight?*

356. Ernie Roderick – *Welterweight, Middleweight or Light-heavyweight?*

357. Wally Swift – *Lightweight, Welterweight or Middleweight?*

358. Pat Thomas – *Welterweight, Light-middleweight or Middleweight?*

359. Randy Turpin – *Middleweight, Light-heavyweight or Heavyweight?*

360. Matt Wells – *Featherweight, Lightweight or Welterweight?*

ROUND 37
WHAT'S MY NICKNAME? - 1

Which nickname did the following world champions acquire during their careers?

361. Muhammad Ali - The Thinker, Louisville Lip or The Bolt from the Blue?

362. Henry Armstrong - Homicide Hank, The Blaster or The Cloud?

363. Marco Antonio Barrera - Baby Faced Assassin, The Fist or The Glove?

364. Nigel Benn - The Shadow, The Flame or The Dark Destroyer?

365. Chris Byrd - The Burning Lip, The Dancer or Rapid Fire?

366. Roberto Duran - Hands of Fire, Hands of Stone or Hammer Hands?

367. Arturo Gatti – Thunder, Lightning or Storm?

368. Ricky Hatton - The Manchester Powerhouse, The Whirlwind or Hitman?

369. Thomas Hearns – Hitman, Mr Knockout or The Fighting Knight?

370. Bernard Hopkins - The Steelman, The Executioner or The Fireball?

ROUND 38
WHAT'S MY NICKNAME? - 2

371. Jake LaMotta - Bronx Terror, Bronx Bull or Bronx Power?

372. Sergei Lyakhovich - White Wolf, White Dog or White Bear?

373. Barry McGuigan - Clones Storm, Clones Rainfall or Clones Cyclone?

374. Archie Moore - The Craftsman, Old Mongoose or Old Bones?

375. Willie Pep - Will o' the Wisp, Mr Speed or Mr Boxing?

376. John Ruiz - The Quiet Man, Ruthless or The Express?

377. James Toney - Dark Knight, Lights Out or Lights On?

378. Jimmy Wilde - Ghost with a Hammer in his Hand, The Hammer or The Mist?

379. Jess Willard - The Big Man, Pottawatomie Giant or Larger Than Life?

380. Tony Zale - Man of Substance, Man of Iron or Man of Steel?

ROUND 39
WHOSE NICKNAME? – 1

Which boxers acquired the following nicknames?

381. Chop Chop - DeMarcus Corley, Johnny Tapia or Leonardo Dorin?

382. Iron Mike - Mike Tyson, Mike McTigue or Mike Weaver?

383. Little Chocolate - Henry Armstrong, Sandy Saddler or George Dixon?

384. Little Stone - Steve Forbes, Juan Molina or Floyd Mayweather Jr?

385. Popo - Shane Mosley, Acelino Freitas or Manuel Medina?

386. Smoke - Chris Eubank, Derrick Gainer or Ike Williams?

387. Smoking Joe - Joe Lynch, Joe Frazier or Joe Bowker?

388. Sweet C - Colin McMillan, Curtis Cokes or Charlie Magri?

389. Terrible Terry - Terry Norris, Terry McGovern or Terry Marsh?

390. The Terrible - Érik Morales, Alexander Muñoz or Nelson Dieppa?

ROUND 40
WHOSE NICKNAME? - 2

391. Black Uhlan - Max Schmeling, Mickey Walker or John Henry Lewis?

392. Brown Bomber - Dwight Muhammad Qwai, Joe Louis or Bob Foster?

393. Cuban Bon Bon - Kid Chocolate, Luis Rodríguez or Kid Gavilan?

394. Durable Dane - Gert Bo Jacobsen, Battling Nelson or Johnny Bredahl?

395. Fighting Marine - Byron Mitchell, Bobby Czyz or Gene Tunney?

396. Ghetto Wizard - Benny Leonard, Beau Jack or Tony Canzoneri?

397. The Ghost - Jim Watt, Roy Jones Jr or Robert Guerrero?

398. Mighty Atom - Rubén Olivares, Jimmy Wilde or Yoddamrong Sithyodthong?

399. Pittsburgh Kid - Frankie Randall, Maurice Blocker or Billy Conn?

400. Whitechapel Whirlwind - Jack (Kid) Berg, Ted (Kid) Lewis or John H. Stracey?

ROUND 41
COMMONWEALTH CHAMPIONS - 1

In which weight division did the following boxers win a Commonwealth title in the professional ranks?

401. Monty Betham – Welterweight, Middleweight or Light-heavyweight?

402. Felix Bwalya - Light-welterweight, Welterweight or Middleweight?

403. Lou Cafaro – Middleweight, Super-middleweight or Light-heavyweight?

404. Brian Carr – Flyweight, Bantamweight or Super-bantamweight?

405. Scott Dixon – Lightweight, Light-welterweight or Welterweight?

406. Bobby Dunne – Flyweight, Bantamweight or Featherweight?

407. Lester Ellis – Featherweight, Lightweight or Light-welterweight?

408. Steve Foster – Welterweight, Light-middleweight or Middleweight?

409. Clyde Gray – Welterweight, Light-middleweight or Middleweight?

410. Paul Harvey – Featherweight, Super-featherweight or Lightweight?

ROUND 42
COMMONWEALTH CHAMPIONS – 2

411. Andy Holligan – Lightweight, Light-welterweight or Middleweight?

412. Mickey Hughes – Welterweight, Light-middleweight or Middleweight?

413. Paul Ingle – Flyweight, Bantamweight or Featherweight?

414. Mark Kaylor – Welterweight, Middleweight or Light-heavyweight?

415. Alfred Kotey – Flyweight, Bantamweight or Featherweight?

416. David Kotey – Flyweight, Bantamweight or Featherweight?

417. Tony Laing – Lightweight, Light-welterweight or Welterweight?

418. Steve Muchoki – Flyweight, Bantamweight or Featherweight?

419. Nicky Piper – Middleweight, Super-middleweight or Light-heavyweight?

420. Richie Woodhall – Middleweight, Super-middleweight or Light-heavyweight?

ROUND 43
EUROPEAN CHAMPIONS - 1

In which weight division did the following boxers hold a European title in the professional ranks?

421. Bob Allotey – Bantamweight, Featherweight or Super-featherweight?

422. Fernando Atzori – Flyweight, Bantamweight or Featherweight?

423. Johnny Armour – Flyweight, Bantamweight or Featherweight?

424. Pat Barrett - Light-welterweight, Welterweight or Light-middleweight?

425. Primo Carnera – Middleweight, Light-heavyweight or Heavyweight?

426. Ray Famechon – Bantamweight, Featherweight or Lightweight?

427. Mauro Galvano – Welterweight, Middleweight or Super-middleweight?

428. Jacques Hairabedian – Middleweight, Light-heavy weight or Heavyweight?

429. Prince Naseem Hamed – Bantamweight, Super-bantamweight or Featherweight?

430. Billy Hardy – Featherweight, Super-featherweight or Lightweight?

ROUND 44
EUROPEAN CHAMPIONS - 2

431. Lloyd Honeyghan – Lightweight, Light-welterweight or Welterweight?

432. Ingemar Johansson – Middleweight, Light-heavy weight or Heavyweight?

433. Jean Josselin – Lightweight, Light-welterweight or Welterweight?

434. Paul Lloyd – Flyweight, Bantamweight or Featherweight?

435. Charlie Nash – Lightweight, Welterweight or Middleweight?

436. Johnny Owen – Flyweight, Bantamweight or Featherweight?

437. László Papp – Welterweight, Middleweight or Light-heavyweight?

438. Yvan Prebeg – Middleweight, Light-heavyweight or Heavyweight?

439. Dick Richardson – Middleweight, Light-heavyweight or Heavyweight?

440. Richie Woodhall – Middleweight, Super-middleweight or Light-heavyweight?

ROUND 45
MANAGERS AND PROMOTERS - 1

Match the surname of the managers or promoters with their correct first name

441. Arum – Rob, Bob or Todd?

442. Baker – Bruce, Harry or Jimmy?

443. Berman – Johnny, Anthony or Rodney?

444. Boyce – James, Paul or Claude?

445. Chargin – Don, Ron or Lon?

446. DeGuardia – Jim, Joe or John?

447. DiBella – Lou, Martin or Dean?

448. Feld – Matthew, Jonathan or Edward?

449. Griffin – Johnny, Jimmy or Bobby?

450. Hearn – Alan, Jeff or Barry?

ROUND 46
MANAGERS AND PROMOTERS - 2

451. Hennessy – Kevin, Mick or Nick?

452. King – Ron, Matt or Don?

453. Maloney – Frank, James or David?

454. Mendy – Ted, Ed or Al?

455. Palle – Mads, Kurt or Mogens?

456. Sanigar – Chris, Steven or Tommy?

457. Sauerland – Karl, Wilfried or Gustav?

458. Shaw – Paul, Gary or Ben?

459. Tiftik – Gerard, John or Julien?

460. Warren – John, Jim or Frank?

ROUND 47
PROMOTERS AND MANAGERS - 1

Match the first names of the following promoters or managers with their correct surnames

461. Adam – Fennett, Booth or Long?

462. Alberto – Montano, Litzau or González?

463. Annette – Conroy, Pernel or Foster?

464. Barry – Gill, Hughes or Davis?

465. Brian – Peters, Moore or Costello?

466. Dan – Goossen, Hitching or Kennedy?

467. Dennis – Smith, Hobson or Overton?

468. Dino – Fattina, Salvatore or Duva?

469. Jamie – Calloway, Sanigar or Garside?

470. Jess – Harding, Gregory or Morley?

ROUND 48
PROMOTERS AND MANAGERS - 2

471. Ian – Alan, Pauly or Monroe?

472. Manny – Fernandes, Ruiz or Bazan?

473. Mike – Foster, Salmon or Acri?

474. Murad – Muhammad, Khan or Sasha?

475. Pat – Patterson, Cowdell or Spencer?

476. Philippe – Sidorenko, Fabrice or Fondu?

477. Shelly – Andrews, Finkel or Kandall?

478. Tania – Davis, Clements or Follett?

479. Tommy – James, Gilmour or Moore?

480. Zef – Ramírez, Wolak or Jastrezbski?

ROUND 49
THE LAST CONTEST - 1

Who did the following world champions meet in their last professional contest?

481. Muhammad Ali (heavyweight) - Larry Holmes, Trevor Berbick or Leon Spinks?

482. Nino Benvenuti (light-middleweight and middleweight) - José Chirino, Doyle Baird or Carlos Monzón?

483. John Conteh (WBC light-heavyweight) - James Dixon, Matthew Saad Muhammad or Ivy Brown?

484. Jack Dempsey (heavyweight) - Jack Sharkey, Gene Tunney or Luis Firpo?

485. Sixto Escobar (bantamweight) - Harry Jeffra, Simón Chávez or Frankie Covelli?

486. Tommy Freeman (welterweight) - Billy Hood, Ralph Chong or Jimmy Francis?

487. Emile Griffith (welterweight, middleweight and light-middleweight-Austrian) - Alan Minter, Joel Bonnetaz or Mayfield Pennington?

488. Ingemar Johansson (heavyweight) - Dick Richardson, Joe Bygraves or Brian London?

489. Rocky Kansas (lightweight) - Joe Trippe, Sammy Mandell or Pal Moran?

490. Benny Lynch (flyweight) - Aurel Toma, Kayo Morgan or Jackie Jurich?

ROUND 50
THE LAST CONTEST - 2

491. Joey Maxim (light-heavyweight) - Mino Bozzano, Ulli Ritter or Heinz Neuhaus?

492. Freddie Miller (featherweight) - Herschel Joiner, Georgie Hansford or Simón Chávez?

493. Ken Overlin (middleweight) - R.J. Lewis, Paul Hartneck or John Donnelly?

494. Paul Pender (middleweight) - Sugar Ray Robinson, Carmen Basilio or Terry Downes?

495. Andre Routis (featherweight) - Davey Abad, Battling Battalino or Johnny Datto?

496. Petey Sarron (featherweight) - Yucatan Kid, Sammy Angott or Wishy Jones?

497. Young Jack Thompson (welterweight) - Leonard Bennett, Charlie Cobb or Al Trulmans?

498. Jim Watt (WBC lightweight) - Alexis Arguello, Sean O'Grady or Howard Davis?

499. Howard Winstone (WBC featherweight) - Jimmy Anderson, José Legrá or Mitsunori Seki?

500. Tony Zale (middleweight) - Marcel Cerdan, Rocky Graziano or Lou Woods?

ROUND 51
SUGAR RAY ROBINSON WINS WORLD WELTERWEIGHT TITLE

501. Sugar Ray Robinson won the vacant world welterweight title on 20 December 1946 when he defeated opponent Tommy Bell by which method - 6 round stoppage, 8 round knockout or 15 round points decision?

502. Who was the referee of the Robinson v. Bell contest - Eddie Joseph, Jackie Davis or Johnny Weber?

503. In which American city did the Robinson v. Bell contest take place – Pittsburgh, New York or Los Angeles?

504. On 8 September 1947 Freddie Mills won the vacant European light-heavyweight title when Paul Goffaux retired in which round – 4, 5 or 6?

505. Ezzard Charles retained his world heavyweight title on 7 March 1951 when he outpointed challenger Jersey Joe Walcott over 15 rounds. Who was the referee - Ruby Goldstein, Clarence Rosen or Mark Conn?

506. At the time of the Charles v. Walcott contest, who was the British and Empire heavyweight champion - Johnny Williams, Bruce Woodcock or Jack Gardner?

507. On 11 June 1951 former world and European flyweight champion Terry Allen won the vacant British flyweight crown when he defeated Vic Herman by which method - 4 round stoppage, 9 round knockout or 15 round points decision?

508. At this stage of his career Terry Allen had participated in how many professional contests – 63, 64 or 65?

509. On 26 October 1951 Rocky Marciano knocked out former world heavyweight champion Joe Louis in which round – 8, 9 or 10?

510. At this stage of his career Rocky Marciano was now undefeated in how many professional contests – 37, 38 or 39?

ROUND 52
ROCKY MARCIANO BECOMES NEW WORLD HEAVYWEIGHT CHAMP

511. During his reign as world heavyweight champion Joe Louis made how many successful defences of the title – 25, 26 or 27?
512. Kid Gavilan retained his world welterweight title on 4 February 1952 when he outpointed Bobby Dykes over 15 rounds in a contest held in which American city – Philadelphia, New York or Miami?
513. Rocky Marciano won the world heavyweight title on 23 September 1952 when he knocked out holder Jersey Joe Walcott in which round – 11, 12 or 13?
514. Who was the referee of the Marciano v. Walcott contest - Zack Clayton, Charley Daggert or Harry Kessler?
515. Sandy Saddler retained his world featherweight title on 25 February 1955 against challenger Teddy Davis by which method - 4 round knockout, 15 round points decision or A draw?
516. Rocky Marciano retained the world heavyweight title on 21 September 1955 when he knocked out challenger Archie Moore in which round – 7, 8 or 9?
517. Rocky Marciano retired from boxing having won how many of his professional contests inside the distance– 42, 43 or 44?
518. Pat McAteer retained his Empire middleweight title on 12 November 1955 when he defeated challenger Mike Holt by which method - 3 round stoppage, 9 round knockout or 15 round points decision?
519. In which country did the McAteer v. Holt contest take place - South Africa, England or Australia?
520. Mario D'Agata won the NY/ EBU version of the world bantamweight title on 29 June 1956 when defending champion Robert Cohen retired in which round – 4, 5 or 6?

ROUND 53
HENRY COOPER FAILS IN EUROPEAN HEAVYWEIGHT CHALLENGE

521. Dick Tiger defeated Terry Downes on 14 May 1957 by which method - 4 round stoppage, 5 round knockout or 6 round retirement?
522. Henry Cooper failed in his bid to win the European heavyweight title on 19 May 1957 when he was knocked out by defending champion Ingemar Johansson in which round – 4, 5 or 6?
523. In which country did the Cooper v. Johansson contest take place – France, Denmark or Sweden?
524. On 17 March 1958 Albert Finch was knocked out in the third round by Noel Trigg. How many bouts had Finch participated during his career – 103, 104 or 105?
525. Who did Manuel González outpoint over 10 rounds on 27 April 1959 - José Nápoles, Curtis Cokes or Luis Rodríguez?
526. Pone Kingpetch won the world flyweight title when he defeated defending champion Pascual Pérez by which method on 16 April 1960 - 6 round stoppage, 9 round knockout or 15 round points decision?
527. In which country did the Kingpetch v. Pérez contest take place – Thailand, Argentina or Japan?
528. Henry Cooper retained his British and Empire heavyweight titles on 21 March 1961 when he defeated challenger Joe Erskine by which method - 4 round stoppage, 5 round retirement or 6 round knockout?
529. True or false: Joe Erskine was a former holder of the British heavyweight title?
530. Billy Backus met opponent Billy Anderson in a 10 round contest on 30 October 1964. What was the result - A points win for Anderson, A points win for Backus or A draw?

ROUND 54
HOWARD WINSTONE WINS VACANT WBC WORLD FEATHERWEIGHT TITLE

531. Muhammad Ali retained his world heavyweight title on 25 May 1965 when he knocked out challenger and former champion Sonny Liston in which round – 1, 2 or 3?
532. In which American city did the Ali v. Liston contest take place - Las Vegas, Houston or Lewiston?
533. British and Empire bantamweight champion Alan Rudkin failed in his bid when challenging for the world championship in the division against defending champion Fighting Harada on 30 November 1965. By which method was Rudkin defeated - 5 round stoppage, 8 round knockout or 15 round points decision?
534. In which country did the Harada v. Rudkin contest take place – England, Japan or Australia?
535. Which former boxer won the ABA heavyweight title in 1961 - Johnny Prescott, Billy Aird or Billy Walker?
536. Ken Buchanan outpointed opponent Tommy Tiger over eight rounds on 24 January 1966. At this stage of his career Buchanan was now undefeated in how many professional bouts – 6, 7 or 8?
537. Johnny Pritchett retained his British middleweight title on 20 February 1967 when he outpointed challenger Wally Swift over 15 rounds. At this stage of his career Pritchett was now undefeated in how many professional contests – 24, 25 or 26?
538. Howard Winstone won the vacant WBC world featherweight title on 23 January 1968 when he stopped opponent Mitsunori Seki in which round – 7, 8 or 9?
539. Who was the referee of the Winstone v. Seki contest - Roland Dakin, George Smith or Wally Thom?
540. At this stage of his career Howard Winstone had now participated in how many professional contests – 63, 64 or 65?

ROUND 55
KEN BUCHANAN WINS WBA WORLD LIGHTWEIGHT TITLE

541. Susumu Hanagata retained his Japanese flyweight title on 12 April 1970 when he defeated challenger Seiichi Watanuki by which method - 4 round stoppage, 6 round knockout or 10 round points decision?

542. Over how many rounds did John H. Stracey outpoint opponent David Pesenti on 12 May 1970 – 6, 8 or 10?

543. On 26 September 1970 Ken Buchanan won the WBA world lightweight title when he defeated Ismael Laguna by which method - 8 round stoppage, 9 round knockout or 15 round points decision?

544. In which country did the Laguna v. Buchanan contest take place - Puerto Rico, Colombia or Panama?

545. Who was the referee of the Laguna v. Buchanan contest - Lee Grossman, Waldemar Schmidt or Ray Solis?

546. On 16 March 1971 Joe Bugner won the British, European and Commonwealth heavyweight titles when he defeated defending champion Henry Cooper by which method - 9 round stoppage, 12 round knock out or 15 round points decision?

547. John McCluskey lost his Commonwealth flyweight title on 6 August 1971 to challenger Henry Nissen when he retired in which round – 7, 8 or 9?

548. In which country did the McCluskey v. Nissen contest take place – Australia, Canada or Jamaica?

549. José Nápoles retained his world welterweight title on 28 March 1972 when he knocked out challenger Ralph Charles in which round – 5, 6 or 7?

550. Who was the referee of the Nápoles v. Charles contest - Dick Young, James Brimmell or Jay Edson?

ROUND 56
CARLOS MONZÓN REIGNS SUPREME

551. On 3 May 1972 Jim Watt won the vacant British lightweight title when he stopped Tony Riley in which round - 12, 13 or 14?

552. Where did the Watt v. Riley contest take place – Solihull, Leeds or Glasgow?

553. At this stage of his career Jim Watt had participated in how many professional contests -15, 16 or 17?

554. Roberto Duran won the WBA world lightweight title on 26 June 1972 when he stopped defending champion Ken Buchanan in which round – 12, 13 or 14?

555. In which American city did the Buchanan v. Duran contest take place - New York, Los Angeles or Boston?

556. Who was the referee of the Buchanan v. Duran contest - Rudy Jordan, John LoBianco or Lee Grossman?

557. On 11 November 1972 Carlos Monzón retained his world middleweight title when he defeated challenger Bennie Briscoe by which method - 8 round retirement, 10 round knockout or 15 round points decision?

558. Who was the referee of the Monzón v. Briscoe contest - Victor Avendaño, Harry Gibbs or Pierrot Brenbilla?

559. In which country did the Monzón v. Briscoe contest take place – Italy, Argentina or France?

560. How many successful defences of the world middleweight title had Carlos Monzón now made – 4, 5 or 6?

ROUND 57
JOHN CONTEH WINS VACANT WORLD LIGHT-HEAVYWEIGHT TITLE

561. Ken Buchanan regained his British lightweight title on 29 January 1973 when he defeated defending champion Jim Watt by which method - 5 round stoppage, 8 round knockout or 15 round points decision?
562. Where did the Watt v. Buchanan contest take place – Glasgow, Edinburgh or Hamilton?
563. In which round did John Conteh stop opponent Terry Daniels on 14 February 1973 – 4, 5 or 6?
564. Johnny Clark won the vacant European bantamweight title on 17 April 1973 when he defeated opponent Franco Zurlo by which method - 5 round knockout, 8 round stoppage or 15 round points decision?
565. In defence of his world heavyweight title on 26 March 1974 George Foreman stopped challenger Ken Norton in which round – 1, 2 or 3?
566. On 21 May 1974 John Conteh retained his British, European and Commonwealth light-heavyweight titles when he stopped challenger and former champion Chris Finnegan in which round – 4, 5 or 6?
567. John Conteh won the vacant WBC world light-heavyweight title on 1 October 1974 when he defeated Jorge Ahumada by which method - 6 round stoppage, 8 round knockout or 15 round points decision?
568. In which country did the Conteh v. Ahumada contest take place – England, France or Argentina?
569. Who was the referee of the Conteh v. Ahumada contest - Waldemar Schmidt, Harry Gibbs or Stan Christodoulou?
570. Susumu Hanagata won the WBA world flyweight title on 18 October 1974 when he stopped defending champion Chartchai Chionoi in which round – 6, 7 or 8?

ROUND 58
JOHN H. STRACEY WINS WBC WORLD WELTERWEIGHT TITLE

571. Jim Watt regained the British lightweight championship on 27 January 1975 when he stopped opponent Johnny Cheshire in which round for the vacant crown – 5, 6 or 7?
572. Maurice Hope stopped opponent Don Cobbs in which round on 11 February 1975 – 3, 4 or 5?
573. At this stage of his career Maurice Hope had participated in 13 professional bouts, but how many had he won -10, 11 or 12?
574. Guts Ishimatsu retained his WBC world lightweight title on 27 February 1975 when he outpointed which challenger over 15 rounds - Ken Buchanan, Tury Pineda or Rodolfo González?
575. Joe Bugner failed to win the world heavyweight title on 1 July 1975 when defending champion Muhammad Ali outpointed him over 15 rounds. At this stage of his career how many times had Bugner travelled the full distance of 15 rounds – 4, 5 or 6?
576. Larry Holmes outpointed opponent Charlie James over 10 rounds on 26 August 1975. At this stage of his professional career Holmes was now undefeated in how many bouts – 16, 17 or 18?
577. José Nápoles lost his WBC world welterweight title on 6 December 1975 when John H. Stracey stopped him in which round – 6, 7 or 8?
578. In which country did the Nápoles v. Stracey contest take place – America, Mexico or England?
579. Who was the referee of the Nápoles v. Stracey contest - Octavio Meyran, Ramón Berumen or Isidoro Rodríguez?
580. At this stage of his professional career John H. Stracey had now participated in how many professional bouts – 45, 46 or 47?

ROUND 59
MUHAMMAD ALI REMAINS KING OF THE HEAVYWEIGHT DIVISION

581. Vito Antuofermo won the European light-middleweight title on 16 January 1976 when he defeated defending champion Eckhard Dagge by which method - 5 round knockout, 8 round retirement or 15 round points decision?
582. In which country did the Dagge v. Antuofermo contest take place – France, West Germany or Italy?
583. On 24 January 1976 Billy Backus outpointed opponent Pablo Rodríguez over how many rounds – 6, 8 or 10?
584. In which weight division did Billy Backus once hold a world title – Lightweight, Welterweight or Middleweight?
585. Bunny Sterling won the vacant European middleweight title on 20 February 1976 when he stopped opponent Frank Reiche in which round – 13, 14 or 15?
586. In which country did the Sterling v. Reiche contest take place – England, France or West Germany?
587. John H. Stracey retained his WBC world welterweight title on 20 March 1976 when he stopped challenger Hedgemon Lewis in which round – 9, 10 or 11?
588. Alfonso Zamora retained his WBA world bantamweight title on 3 April 1976 when he knocked out challenger Eusebio Pedroza in which round – 1, 2 or 3?
589. Muhammad Ali retained his world heavyweight title on 25 May 1976 when he stopped challenger Richard Dunn in which round – 5, 6 or 7?
590. Eckhard Dagge won the WBC world light-middleweight title on 18 June 1976 when defending champion Elisha Obed retired in which round – 8, 9 or 10?

ROUND 60
JOHN CONTEH RETAINS WBC WORLD LIGHT-HEAVYWEIGHT TITLE

591. Which role did George Parnassus play in boxing – Referee, Judge or Promoter?
592. Carlos Palomino captured the WBC world welterweight title on 22 June 1976 when he stopped defending champion John H. Stracey in which round – 12, 13 or 14?
593. Who was the referee of the Stracey v. Palomino contest - Harry Gibbs, Sid Nathan or Dick Young?
594. Muhammad Ali retained his world heavyweight title on 28 September 1976 when he outpointed challenger Ken Norton over 15 rounds. In which American city did this contest take place - Las Vegas, New York or Boston?
595. On 9 October 1976 John Conteh retained his WBC world light-heavyweight title against challenger Yaqui López by which method - 5 round stoppage, 8 round knockout or 15 round points decision?
596. In which country did the Conteh v. López contest take place – England, Denmark or America?
597. On 5 November 1976 Danny 'Little Red' López won the WBC world featherweight title when he outpointed holder David Kotey over 15 rounds. Who was the referee - Harry Gibbs, Ray Solis or Jay Edson?
598. In which country did the Kotey v. López contest take place – Japan, Ghana or America?
599. Dave (Boy) Green won the vacant European light-welterweight title on 7 December 1976 when opponent Jean-Baptiste Piedvache retired in which round – 8, 9 or 10?
600. At this stage of his career Dave (Boy) Green was now undefeated in how many professional contests – 22, 23 or 24?

ROUND 61
ALAN MINTER BECOMES EUROPEAN MIDDLEWEIGHT CHAMPION TITLE

601. Alan Minter won the European middleweight title on 4 February 1977 when he knocked out defending champion Germano Valsecchi in which round – 3, 4 or 5?
602. In which country did the Valsecchi v. Minter contest take place – England, Italy or Spain?
603. On 17 March 1977 George Foreman and Jimmy Young met in a 12 round contest. What was the result - A points win for Foreman, A draw or A points win for Young?
604. Carlos Palomino retained his WBC world welterweight title on 14 June 1977 when he knocked out challenger Dave (Boy) Green in which round – 9, 10 or 11?
605. Jim Watt won the vacant European lightweight title on 5 August 1977 when he stopped opponent Andre Holyk in which round – 1, 2 or 3?
606. On 22 October 1977 Michael Spinks outpointed opponent Gary Summerhays over 8 rounds in a contest in which American city - New York, Atlantic City or Las Vegas?
607. On 4 March 1978 the former British and European middleweight champion Kevin Finnegan met future world middleweight title holder Marvin Hagler but was forced to retire in which round – 6, 7 or 8?
608. In which American city did the Hagler v. Finnegan con test take place - Las Vegas, Boston or New York?
609. On 19 August 1978 future WBA world heavyweight champion Mike Weaver met Leroy Jones in a 12 round contest for the vacant NABF heavyweight title. What was the result - A points win for Jones, A draw or A points win for Weaver?
610. Roberto Castanon retained his European featherweight title on 16 December 1978 when challenger Dave Needham retired in which round – 3, 4 or 5?

ROUND 62
MAURICE HOPE AND JIM WATT BOTH CAPTURE A WORLD TITLE

611. Maurice Hope won the WBC world light-middleweight title on 4 March 1979 when defending champion Rocky Mattioli retired in which round – 7, 8 or 9?

612. In which country did the Mattioli v. Hope contest take place – Italy, Australia or England?

613. Who was the referee of the Mattioli v. Hope contest - Paul Field, Dick Young or Ray Solis?

614. Jim Watt won the vacant WBC world lightweight title on 17 April 1979 when he stopped opponent Alfredo Pitalua in which round -12, 13 or 14?

615. In which part of Scotland did the Watt v. Pitalua contest take place – Hamilton, Edinburgh or Glasgow?

616. Who was the referee of the Watt v. Pitalua contest - Arthur Mercante, Isidoro Rodríguez or Tony Pérez?

617. On 28 September 1979 Roberto Duran outpointed opponent Zeferino González over 10 rounds in a contest in which American city - New York, Las Vegas or Detroit?

618. On 30 November 1979 Thomas Hearns outpointed Mike Colbert over 10 rounds. At this stage of his career he was now undefeated in how many professional contests – 23, 24 or 25?

619. Charlie Nash retained his European lightweight title on 6 December 1979 when he defeated challenger Ken Buchanan by which method - 5 round stoppage, 7 round knockout or 12 round points decision?

620. On 8 December 1979 Pipino Cuevas retained his WBA world welterweight title by stopping challenger Ángel Espada in which round – 10, 11 or 12?

ROUND 63
MARVIN HAGLER WINS UNDISPUTED WORLD MIDDLEWEIGHT TITLE

621. On 3 February 1980 Larry Holmes retained his WBC world heavyweight title when he knocked out challenger Lorenzo Zanon in which round – 4, 5 or 6?

622. In which part of America did the Holmes v. Zanon contest take place - Las Vegas, New York or Houston?

623. On 31 March 1980 Sugar Ray Leonard retained his WBC world welterweight title when he knocked out challenger Dave (Boy) Green in which round – 3, 4 or 5?

624. On 16 March 1980 Vito Antuofermo lost his world middleweight title to Alan Minter when he was defeated by which method - 5 round stoppage, 8 round knockout or 15 round points decision?

625. In which country did the Antuofermo v. Minter contest take place – Italy, America or England?

626. On 17 April 1980 Jorgen Hansen retained his European welterweight title when he defeated challenger Joey Singleton by which method - 6 round stoppage, 8 round knockout or 12 round points decision?

627. On 17 May 1980 Marvin Hagler outpointed opponent Marcos Geraldo over how many rounds – 8, 10 or 12?

628. On 27 September 1980 Marvin Hagler won the world middleweight title when he stopped defending champion Alan Minter in which round – 1, 2 or 3?

629. In which country did the Minter v. Hagler contest take place – England, America or Canada?

630. Who was the referee of the Minter v. Hagler contest - Mills Lane, David Pearl or Carlos Berrocal?

ROUND 64
SEAN O'GRADY BECOMES NEW WBA WORLD LIGHTWEIGHT KING

631. At the stage of his victory over Alan Minter, Marvin Hagler had now participated in how many professional contests – 53, 54 or 55?
632. In defence of his WBC world lightweight title on 1 November 1980 Jim Watt stopped challenger Sean O'Grady in which round – 10, 11 or 12?
633. Lupe Pintor retained his WBC world bantamweight title on 22 February 1981 when he outpointed challenger José Uziga over 15 rounds in a contest in which American city – Houston, Las Vegas or Los Angeles?
634. On 24 February 1981 Charlie Magri retained his European flyweight championship title when he stopped challenger Enrique Rodríguez in round two. How many times had Magri now defended his title – 1, 2 or 3?
635. On 17 March 1981 Sean O'Grady defeated opponent José Cabrera when he outpointed him over how many rounds – 8, 10 or 12?
636. On 3 April 1981 Jorge Herrera and Eleoncio Mercedes met in a 10 round contest. What was the result - A points win for Herrera, A draw or A points win for Mercedes?
637. Sean O'Grady won the WBA world lightweight title when he defeated holder Hilmer Kenty by which method - 6 round knockout, 8 round stoppage or 15 round points decision?
638. Wilfred Benítez won the WBC world light-middleweight title on 24 May 1981 when he knocked out defending champion Maurice Hope in which round – 12, 13 or 14?
639. In which country did the Hope v. Benítez contest take place – England, America or Denmark?
640. Who was the referee of the Hope v. Benítez contest - David Pearl, Richard Greene or Robert Ferrara?

ROUND 65: TONY SIBSON FAILS TO WIN WORLD MIDDLEWEIGHT TITLE

641. On 15 September 1981 Alan Minter failed to regain the European middleweight title when defending champion Tony Sibson knocked him out in which round – 1, 2 or 3?
642. On 24 November 1981 former world bantamweight and featherweight champion Rubén Olivares met opponent Margarito Márquez in a 10 round contest. What was the result - A points win for Olivares, A draw or A points win for Márquez?
643. Future WBC world featherweight title holder Juan La Porte failed in his challenge for the WBA version of the crown on 24 January 1982 when defending champion Eusebio Pedroza defeated him by which method - 5 round stoppage, 6 round knockout or 15 round points decision?
644. In which American city did the Pedroza v. La Porte contest take place - Atlantic City, New York or Boston?
645. Who was the referee of the Pedroza v. La Porte contest - Tony Pérez, Guy Jutras or Stan Christoudoulou?
646. On 11 February 1983 Tony Sibson failed in his challenge for the world middleweight title when defending champion Marvin Hagler stopped him in which round – 6, 7 or 8?
647. In which country did the Hagler v. Sibson contest take place – England, Canada or America?
648. On 3 May 1983 Frank Bruno stopped opponent Scott LeDoux in three rounds. At this stage of his career Bruno was now undefeated in how many professional contests – 15, 16 or 17?
649. British featherweight champion Barry McGuigan won the vacant European title on 16 November 1983 when he knocked out opponent Valerio Nati in which round – 5, 6 or 7?
650. Which of the following boxers did not challenge for the world heavyweight title during their respective professional careers - Jerry Quarry, Randall (Tex) Cobb or John L. Gardner?

ROUND 66
A HEAVYWEIGHT CALLED MIKE TYSON LOOKS A FUTURE CHAMP

651. In which country did former world light-heavyweight champion Bob Foster not box during his professional career - South Africa, England or Switzerland?
652. On 15 January 1984 Duke McKenzie outpointed David Capo over four rounds in a contest in which country – America, England or Italy?
653. On 15 June 1984 Thomas Hearns retained his WBC world light-middleweight title when he knocked out challenger Roberto Duran in which round – 1, 2 or 3?
654. Marvin Hagler retained his world middleweight title on 19 October 1984 when he stopped Mustafa Hamsho in which round – 3, 4 or 5?
655. On 5 June 1985 Duke McKenzie won the vacant British flyweight title when he stopped Danny Flynn in which round - 4, 5 or 6?
656. Barry McGuigan won the WBA world featherweight title when he defeated defending champion Eusebio Pedroza on 8 June 1985 by a 15 round points decision in a contest in which country – America, Panama or England?
657. Hector Camacho won the WBC world lightweight title on 10 August 1985 when he defeated defending champion José Luis Ramírez by which method - 6 round stoppage, 8 round knockout or 12 round points decision?
658. On 13 November 1985 Mike Tyson stopped Eddie Richardson in round one. At this stage of his professional career, how many bouts had Tyson now won in the opening round – 9, 10 or 11?
659. After the Richardson victory Tyson was now undefeated in how many professional contests – 10, 11 or 12?
660. In which American city did the Tyson v. Richardson contest take place – Houston, Las Vegas or New York?

ROUND 67
HONEYGHAN WINS AGAINST THE ODDS

661. Tim Witherspoon won the WBA version of the world heavyweight title on 17 January 1986 when he defeated defending champion Tony Tubbs by which method - 8 round stoppage, 10 round knockout or 15 round points decision?
662. In which American city did the Witherspoon v. Tubbs contest take place – Atlanta, New York or Las Vegas?
663. On 10 March 1986 Marvin Hagler retained his world middleweight crown when he knocked out challenger John Mugbai in which round – 10, 11 or 12?
664. How many successful defences of the world middleweight title had Hagler now made – 10, 11 or 12?
665. Lloyd Honeyghan won the world welterweight title on 27 September 1986 when defending champion Don Curry retired in which round – 6, 7 or 8?
666. Prior to the Honeyghan contest Curry had made how many successful defences of the world welterweight title – 7, 8 or 9?
667. In which country did the Honeyghan v. Curry contest take place – England, America or Italy?
668. At this stage of his career Honeyghan was now undefeated in how many professional contests – 27, 28 or 29?
669. Terry Marsh won the IBF world light-welterweight title on 4 March 1987 when he defeated defending champion Joe Manley by which method - 3 round retirement, 6 round stoppage or 10 round stoppage?
670. On 24 July 1987 former European, British and Commonwealth heavyweight champion Joe Bugner defeated former world champion Greg Page by which method - 6 round knockout, 8 round stoppage or 10 round points decision?

ROUND 68
NIGEL BENN BECOMES NEW COMMONWEALTH MIDDLEWEIGHT CHAMP

671. Which version of the world heavyweight championship did Greg Page once hold – WBA, WBC or IBF?
672. In which country did the Joe Bugner v. Greg Page contest take place – England, America or Australia?
673. On 10 September 1987 Gary De'Roux stopped opponent Colin Lynch in three rounds. In how many professional contests had De Roux now participated – 7, 8 or 9?
674. Nigel Benn knocked out opponent Ian Chantler in the first round on 24 November 1987. How many times had Benn now won in the opening round – 7, 8 or 9?
675. At this stage of his career Nigel Benn was now undefeated in how many professional contests – 10, 11 or 12?
676. In defence of his WBC world flyweight title on 31 January 1988 Sot Chitalada stopped challenger Hideaki Kamishiro in which round – 6, 7 or 8?
677. On 21 March 1988 Mike Tyson retained his world heavyweight title when he stopped challenger Tony Tubbs in which round – 1, 2 or 3?
678. In which country did the Tyson v. Tubbs contest take place – Japan, America or Germany?
679. Nigel Benn won the vacant Commonwealth middleweight title on 28 April 1988 when he stopped opponent Abdul Amoru Sanda in which round – 1, 2 or 3?
680. Chris Eubank stopped opponent Steve Aquilina in round four on 18 May 1988. At this stage of his career Eubank was now undefeated in how many professional contests – 8, 9 or 10?

ROUND 69
CHRIS EUBANK CONTINUES UNDEFEATED RUN

681. On 27 November 1988 Sung-II Moon retained his WBA world bantamweight title when he knocked out challenger Edgar Monserrat in which round – 6, 7 or 8?

682. Mike McCallum retained his WBA world middleweight title on 10 May 1989 when he defeated challenger Herol Graham by which method - 4 round stoppage, 8 round knockout or 12 round points decision?

683. In which country did the McCallum v. Graham title bout take place – England, America or France?

684. Nigel Benn lost his Commonwealth middleweight title on 21 May 1989 when challenger Michael Watson knocked him out in which round – 5, 6 or 7?

685. In which round did Colin McMillan stop opponent Miguel Matthews on 12 June 1989 – 1, 2 or 3?

686. In which round did Chris Eubank knock out opponent Johnny Melfah on 5 November 1989 – 3, 4 or 5?

687. Where did the Eubank v. Melfah contest take place – London, Manchester or Liverpool?

688. At this stage of his career Chris Eubank was now undefeated in how many professional contests – 17, 18 or 19?

689. On 29 November 1989 Gary De'Roux knocked out opponent James Hunter in which round – 2, 3 or 4?

690. In how many professional bouts had Gary De Roux now participated -12, 13 or 14?

ROUND 70
JAMES DOUGLAS DEFEATS MIKE TYSON TO WIN WORLD HEAVYWEIGHT TITLE

691. On 11 February 1990 James (Buster) Douglas won the world heavyweight title when he knocked out defending champion Mike Tyson in which round – 9, 10 or 11?
692. In which country did the Tyson v. Douglas contest take place – Japan, America or Australia?
693. Who was the referee of the Tyson v. Douglas contest - Octavio Meyran, Mills Lane or Arthur Mercante?
694. On 9 May 1990 Lennox Lewis defeated opponent Jorgé Dascola by a knockout in round one. How many times had Lewis now won in the opening round – 3, 4 or 5?
695. At this stage of his career Lennox Lewis was now undefeated in how many professional contests – 8, 9 or 10?
696. On 28 May 1990 Jean Chanet retained his European heavyweight title when he defeated Derek Williams by which method - 2 round knockout, 4 round retirement or 12 round points decision?
697. In which country did the Chanet v. Williams contest take place – Italy, England or France?
698. Lennox Lewis won the European heavyweight title on 31 October 1990 when he stopped defending champion Jean Chanet in which round – 6, 7 or 8?
699. Lennox Lewis was now undefeated in how many professional contests -14, 15 or 16?
700. On 8 December 1990 Julio César Chávez retained his world WBC and IBF light-welterweight titles when he stopped challenger Kyung-Duk Ahn in which round – 1, 2 or 3?

ROUND 71
DAVE McAULEY RETAINS IBF WORLD FLYWEIGHT TITLE

701. Terry Norris retained his WBC world light-middleweight title on 9 February 1991 when he defeated challenger Sugar Ray Leonard by which method - 3 round knockout, 8 round retirement or 12 round points decision?
702. In which American city did the Norris v. Leonard contest take place - New York, Las Vegas or Washington DC?
703. At this stage of his career Sugar Ray Leonard had now participated in how many professional contests – 38, 39 or 40?
704. Gary De'Roux won the British featherweight title on 5 March 1991 when he knocked out holder Sean Murphy in which round – 3, 4 or 5?
705. In which round did Felix Trinidad stop opponent Felix Vazquez on 1 May 1991 – 1, 2 or 3?
706. On 11 May 1991 Dave McAuley retained his IBF world flyweight title when he defeated challenger Pedro Feliciano by which method - 3 round retirement, 6 round knockout or 12 round points decision?
707. How many times had Dave McAuley now successfully defended the IBF crown – 3, 4 or 5?
708. On 22 May 1991 Colin McMillan won the British featherweight title when he stopped defending champion Gary De'Roux in which round – 6, 7 or 8?
709. At this stage of his career Colin McMillan had now participated in how many professional contests – 18, 19 or 20?
710. On 23 September 1991 Bernard Hopkins stopped opponent Ralph Moncrief in the opening round. How many professional bouts had Hopkins now won in the first round – 8, 9 or 10?

ROUND 72
PAT CLINTON WINS WBO WORLD FLYWEIGHT TITLE

711. Former WBC and IBF heavyweight champion Larry Holmes met opponent Jamie Howe on 12 November 1991 and stopped him in which round – 1, 2 or 3?
712. Jeff Fenech failed in his attempt to win the WBC world super-featherweight title on 1 March 1992 when defending champion Azumah Nelson stopped him in which round – 7, 8 or 9?
713. In which country did the Nelson v. Fenech contest take place – America, Ghana or Australia?
714. Which version of the world bantamweight title did Jeff Fenech previously hold – WBC, WBA or IBF?
715. In which round did Chris Pyatt stop challenger James Tapisha in defence of his Commonwealth light-middleweight title on 28 April 1992 – 1, 2 or 3?
716. Riddick Bowe stopped opponent Everett Martin in round five on 8 May 1992 and was now undefeated in how many professional contests – 28, 29 or 30?
717. Pat Clinton won the WBO world flyweight title on 18 March 1992 when he defeated defending champion Isidro Pérez by which method - 5 round stoppage, 8 round knockout or 12 round points decision?
718. Where did the Clinton v. Pérez contest take place – Glasgow, Cardiff or Manchester?
719. In how many professional contests had Pat Clinton now participated – 18, 19 or 20?
720. Prior to Pat Clinton, who was the last boxer from Scotland to hold a version of the world flyweight title - Jackie Paterson, Benny Lynch or Walter McGowan?

ROUND 73
LENNOX LEWIS AND FRANK BRUNO MEET FOR WORLD HEAVYWEIGHT TITLE

721. Lennox Lewis stopped opponent Mike Dixon in which round on 11 August 1992 – 3, 4 or 5?
722. In which country did the Lewis v. Nixon contest take place – England, Canada or America?
723. At this stage of his career Lennox Lewis was now undefeated in how many professional contests – 21, 22 or 23?
724. In which round did Oscar De La Hoya knock out opponent Cliff Hicks on 12 December 1992 – 1, 2 or 3?
725. Nigel Benn retained his WBC world super-middleweight title against former title holder Mauro Galvano on 6 March 1993 when he defeated him by which method - 8 round knockout, 9 round retirement or 12 round points decision?
726. Where did the Benn v. Galvano contest take place – London, Glasgow or Cardiff?
727. On 1 October 1993 Lennox Lewis retained his WBC world heavyweight title against challenger Frank Bruno when he stopped him in which round – 7, 8 or 9?
728. Where did the Lewis v. Bruno contest take place – London, Cardiff or Manchester?
729. True or false: the Lewis v. Bruno contest was notable since it was the first time that two British fighters had fought each other for a version of the world heavy weight title?
730. This was the third time that Frank Bruno had challenged for the world heavyweight title. The first challenge took place on 19 July 1986 when the then WBA champion Tim Witherspoon stopped him in which round – 10, 11 or 12?

ROUND 74
PRINCE NASEEM HAMED RETAINS TITLE

731. Frank Bruno's second attempt to win the world heavy weight title took place on 25 February 1989 when the defending WBC champion Mike Tyson stopped him in which round – 4, 5 or 6?
732. Steve Robinson retained his WBO world featherweight title on 12 March 1994 when he knocked out challenger Paul Hodkinson in which round – 10, 11 or 12?
733. Which version of the world featherweight title did Paul Hodkinson previously hold –WBC, WBA or IBF?
734. Chris Eubank retained his WBO world super-middleweight title on 21 May 1994 when he defeated challenger Ray Close by which method - 6 round knockout, 8 round retirement or 12 round points decision?
735. Pernell Whitaker retained his WBC world welterweight title on 1October 1994 when he defeated challenger Buddy McGirt by which method - 6 round knockout, 9 round retirement or 12 round points decision?
736. Bernard Hopkins and Segundo Mercado contested the vacant IBF world middleweight title on 17 December 1994. What was the result - A points win for Hopkins, A draw or A points win for Mercado?
737. On 3 January 1995 Tim Austin knocked out opponent Arturo Estrada in which round – 1, 2 or 3?
738. Prince Naseem Hamed retained his WBC international super-bantamweight title against challenger Sergio Liendo on 4 March 1995 when he stopped him in which round – 1, 2 or 3?
739. At this stage of his career Prince Naseem Hamed was now undefeated in how many professional contests – 16, 17 or 18?
740. During his professional career Dennis Andries won which version of the world light-heavyweight title on three separate occasions – IBF, WBC or WBA?

ROUND 75
BERNARD HOPKINS RETAINS IBF WORLD MIDDLEWEIGHT TITLE

741. Johnny Tapia retained his WBO world super-flyweight title on 1 December 1995 when he defeated challenger Willy Salazar who retired in which round – 7, 8 or 9?
742. Which former holder of the British featherweight title boxed in the southpaw stance - Jimmy Revie, Gary De'Roux or Terry Spinks?
743. Robbie Regan won the WBO version of the world bantamweight title on 26 April 1996 when he defeated defending champion Daniel Jiménez by which method - 1 round stoppage, 6 round knockout or 12 round points decision?
744. Akim Tafer won the vacant European cruiserweight title on 25 May 1996 when he stopped opponent Alexei Illin in which round – 4, 5 or 6?
745. Who was the European cruiserweight champion prior to Akim Tafer - Alexander Gurov, Carl Thompson or Patrice Aouissi?
746. Peter Culshaw won the Commonwealth flyweight title on 25 June 1996 when he stopped defending champion Danny Ward in which round – 1, 2 or 3?
747. Who was the referee of the Ward v. Culshaw contest - Richie Davies, Dave Parris or Larry O' Connell?
748. Bernard Hopkins retained his IBF world middleweight title on 16 July 1996 when he stopped challenger Bo James in which round – 10, 11 or 12?
749. In which American city did the Hopkins v. James contest take place – Philadelphia, Atlantic City or Las Vegas?
750. On 22 March 1997 Joe Calzaghe knocked out opponent Tyler Hughes in the first round. How many times in the professional ranks had Calzaghe now won in the opening round – 10, 11 or 12?

ROUND 76
JOE CALZAGHE WINS VACANT WBO SUPER-MIDDLEWEIGHT TITLE

751. Clinton Woods retained his Central Area super-middleweight title on 10 April 1997 when he stopped challenger Darren Littlewood in which round – 4, 5 or 6?
752. Clinton Woods was now undefeated in how many professional contests – 14, 15 or 16?
753. During his professional career which title at super-bantamweight did Spencer Oliver hold – British, World or European?
754. Joe Calzaghe won the vacant WBO world super-middleweight title on 11 October 1997 when he defeated Chris Eubank by which method - 4 round stoppage, 8 round knockout or 12 round points decision?
755. Joe Calzaghe was now undefeated in how many professional contests – 21, 22 or 23?
756. Ricky Hatton defeated opponent Robert Álvarez on 19 December 1997 when he outpointed him over how many rounds – 4, 6 or 7?
757. In which country did the Hatton v. Álvarez contest take place – Germany, England or America?
758. On 19 December 1997 Prince Naseem Hamed retained his WBO world featherweight title when he knocked out Kevin Kelly in which round – 3, 4 or 5?
759. Which version of the world featherweight title did Kevin Kelly previously hold – IBF, WBA or WBC?
760. How many contests did Joe Calzaghe have during 1997 – 3, 4 or 5?

ROUND 77
RICKY HATTON REMAINS UNDEFEATED

761. In which round did Charles Brewer stop challenger Herol Graham in defence of his IBF world super-middleweight title on 28 March 1998 – 9, 10 or 11?
762. In which country did the Brewer v. Graham contest take place – England, America or Italy?
763. On 11 April 1998 Paul Henry made his professional debut, outpointing opponent Lee Simpkin over four rounds. Who was his manager at that time - Frank Maloney, Dai Gardiner or Tania Follett?
764. Prince Naseem Hamed retained his WBO world featherweight title on 18 April 1998 when he stopped challenger and former WBA world champion Wilfredo Vázquez in which round – 7, 8 or 9?
765. Where did the Hamed v. Vázquez contest take place – London, Birmingham or Manchester?
766. At this stage of his career Prince Naseem Hamed was now undefeated in how many professional contests – 29, 30 or 31?
767. On 25 April 1998 Joe Calzaghe retained his WBO world super-middleweight title when challenger Juan Carlos Giménez retired in which round – 7, 8 or 9?
768. On 30 May 1998 Ricky Hatton outpointed opponent Mark Ramsey over how many rounds – 4, 6 or 8?
769. Ricky Hatton was now undefeated in how many professional contests – 5, 6 or 7?
770. Which of the following boxers did British heavyweight contender Billy Walker not meet in the professional ranks during his career - Thad Spencer, Johnny Prescott or Jerry Quarry?

ROUND 78
LEWIS DEFEATS HOLYFIELD IN UNIFICATION CONTEST

771. In which round did Sugar Shane Mosley knock out challenger Wilfredo Ruiz in defence of his IBF world lightweight title on 27 June 1998 – 5, 6 or 7?
772. At this stage of his professional career Sugar Shane Mosley was now undefeated in how many professional contests – 27, 28 or 29?
773. In defence of his WBC world super-middleweight title on 13 February 1999 Richie Woodhall stopped challenger and former holder of the title Vincenzo Nardiello in which round – 6, 7 or 8?
774. Floyd Mayweather Jr retained his WBC world super-featherweight title on 22 May 1999 when he stopped challenger Justin Juuko in which round – 9, 10 or 11?
775. On 29 May 1999 Ricky Hatton won the vacant WBO inter-continental light-welterweight title when he stopped opponent Dillon Carew in which round – 5, 6 or 7?
776. At this stage of his career Ricky Hatton was now undefeated in how many professional contests - 12, 13 or 14?
777. Lennox Lewis retained his WBC world heavyweight title and won the WBA and IBF versions of the title on 13 November 1999 when he defeated Evander Holyfield by which method - 4 round stoppage, 8 round knockout or 12 round points decision?
778. In which country did the Lewis v. Holyfield contest take place – Canada, America or England?
779. In how many professional contests had Lennox Lewis now participated – 37, 38 or 39?
780. In how many world heavyweight title fights had Lennox Lewis now participated – 10, 11 or 12?

ROUND 79
GLENN CATLEY WINS WBC SUPER-MIDDLEWEIGHT WORLD CROWN

781. Johnny Nelson retained his WBO world cruiserweight title on 8 April 2000 when challenger Pietro Aurino retired in which round – 6, 7 or 8?

782. In how many professional contests had Johnny Nelson now participated -50, 51 or 52?

783. On 29 April 2000 Scott Harrison outpointed Tracy Harris Patterson over how many rounds – 8, 10 or 12?

784. In which country did the Harrison v. Patterson contest take place – Canada, England or America?

785. True or false: former two-times world heavyweight champion Floyd Patterson is Tracy Harris Patterson's stepfather?

786. Glenn Catley won the WBC world super-middleweight title on 6 May 2000 when he stopped defending champion Markus Beyer in which round – 10, 11 or 12?

787. In which country did the Catley v. Beyer contest take place – Germany, Italy or England?

788. Cathy Brown won the vacant WBF European flyweight title on 1 July 2000 when she outpointed opponent Jan Wild over how many rounds – 4, 6 or 8?

789. At this stage of her career Cathy Brown was now undefeated in how many professional contests – 3, 4 or 5?

790. Ricky Hatton retained his WBO inter-continental light-welterweight title on 23 September 2000 and also captured the WBA inter-continental light-welterweight crown when he stopped challenger Giuseppe Lauri in which round – 4, 5 or 6?

ROUND 80
JOE CALZAGHE TURNS BACK CHALLENGE OF RICHIE WOODHALL

791. Where did the Ricky Hatton v. Giuseppe Lauri contest take place – London, Manchester or Liverpool?

792. Bernard Hopkins retained his IBF world middleweight title on 1 December 2000 when he stopped challenger Antwun Echols in which round – 10, 11 or 12?

793. In which American city did the Hopkins v. Echols contest take place - New York, Miami or Las Vegas?

794. Colin Lynes outpointed opponent Jimmy Phelan over how many rounds on 9 December 2000 – 4, 6 or 8?

795. At this stage of his career Colin Lynes was now undefeated in how many professional contests – 11, 12 or 13?

796. Which version of the world featherweight title did Paul Ingle once hold – WBC, WBA or IBF?

797. Joe Calzaghe retained his WBO world super-middleweight title on 16 December 2000 when he stopped challenger Richie Woodhall in which round – 9, 10 or 11?

798. Where did the Calzaghe v. Woodhall contest take place – London, Cardiff or Sheffield?

799. Joe Calzaghe was now undefeated in how many professional contests – 29, 30 or 31?

800. How many times did Lennox Lewis defend his world heavyweight title in the year 2000 – 3, 4 or 5?

ROUND 81
LENNOX LEWIS DEFEATED

801. Willie Jorrin retained his WBC world super-bantamweight title on 19 January 2001 when he defeated challenger Oscar Larios by which method - 4 round retirement, 6 round knockout or 12 round points decision?
802. Who did Joe Bugner not meet in the professional ranks - Johnny Prescott, Brian London or Billy Walker?
803. Ricky Hatton won the vacant WBU world light-welterweight title on 26 March 2001 when he knocked out opponent Tony Pep in which round – 3, 4 or 5?
804. Prior to the Pep contest Hatton had won the vacant British light-welterweight title when he defeated opponent Jonathan Thaxton by way of a 12 round points decision. Who held the British crown prior to Hatton - Jason Rowland, Mark Winters or Andy Holligan?
805. Lennox Lewis lost his WBC, IBF and IBO world heavy weight titles on 22 April 2001 when challenger Hasim Rahman knocked him out in which round – 4, 5 or 6?
806. In which country did the Lewis v. Rahman contest take place - South Africa, England or America?
807. On 28 April 2001 Manny Pacquiao knocked out opponent Wetyha Sakmuangkiang in which round – 5, 6 or 7?
808. Felix Trinidad won the WBA world middleweight title on 12 May 2001 when he stopped holder William Joppy in which round - 4, 5 or 7?
809. Which of the following holders of the British heavy weight title did not box in the southpaw stance - Dan McAlinden, Richard Dunn or Jack Bodell?
810. Kostya Tszyu retained his WBC and WBA world light-welterweight titles on 23 June 2001 when he defeated challenger Oktay Urkal by which method - 3 round retirement, 6 round knockout or 12 round points decision?

ROUND 82
JOE CALZAGHE MAKES ANOTHER SUCCESSFUL DEFENCE OF TITLE

811. Danny Williams retained his British and Commonwealth heavyweight titles on 28 July 2001 when he knocked out challenger Julius Francis in which round – 4, 5 or 6?
812. Who was the referee of the Williams v. Francis contest - John Coyle, Mickey Vann or Mark Green?
813. True or false: Julius Francis was a former British and Commonwealth heavyweight champion?
814. During his boxing career, in how many professional contests did Eurosport TV commentator Steve Holdsworth participate – 10, 11 or 12?
815. On 13 October 2001 Joe Calzaghe retained his WBO world super-middleweight title when he stopped challenger Will McIntyre in which round -3, 4 or 5?
816. In which country did the Calzaghe v. McIntyre contest take place – Denmark, Sweden or England?
817. At this stage of his career Joe Calzaghe was now undefeated in how many professional contests – 31, 32 or 33?
818. Lennox Lewis regained the WBC, IBF and IBO world heavyweight titles on 17 November 2001 when he knocked out defending champion Hasim Rahman in which round – 4, 5 or 6?
819. In which country did the Lewis v. Rahman contest take place - South Africa, England or America?
820. At this stage of his career Lennox Lewis had participated in how many professional contests – 41, 42 or 43?

ROUND 83
MIKE TYSON FAILS TO REGAIN WORLD HEAVYWEIGHT TITLE

821. On 13 March 2002 Cathy Brown outpointed opponent Svetla Taskova over how many rounds – 4, 6 or 8?

822. At this stage of her career Cathy Brown had now participated in how many professional contests – 9, 10 or 11?

823. Alex Arthur won the vacant WBO inter-continental super-featherweight title on 8 June 2002 when he defeated opponent Nikolai Eremeev by a retirement in which round – 4, 5 or 6?

824. On 8 June 2002 Lennox Lewis retained his WBC, IBF and IBO world heavyweight titles when he knocked out challenger Mike Tyson in which round – 7, 8 or 9?

825. In which America city did the Lewis v. Tyson contest take place - Las Vegas, Memphis or Atlantic City?

826. On 10 July 2002 Audley Harrison outpointed opponent Dominic Negus over how many rounds – 4, 6 or 8?

827. On 10 July 2002 Nicky Cook outpointed Andrei Devyataykin over how many rounds – 6, 8 or 10?

828. On 20 July 2002 Antonio Tarver stopped opponent Eric Harding in which round – 3, 4 or 5?

829. On 7 September 2002 Roy Jones Jr in defence of his WBC, WBA and IBF world light-heavyweight titles stopped challenger Clinton Woods in which round – 6, 7 or 8?

830. In which country did the Jones Jr v. Woods contest take place – America, France or England?

ROUND 84
ALEX ARTHUR WINS VACANT BRITISH SUPER-FEATHERWEIGHT TITLE

831. Alex Arthur won the vacant British super-featherweight title on 19 October 2002 when he knocked out opponent Steve Conway in which round – 3, 4 or 5?
832. Who was the referee of the Arthur v. Conway contest - Dave Parris, Richie Davies or John Coyle?
833. Alex Arthur was now undefeated in how many professional contests – 11, 12 or 13?
834. Scott Harrison won the WBO world featherweight title on 19 October 2002 when he defeated defending champion Julio Pablo Chacón by which method - 3 round stoppage, 8 round knockout or 12 round points decision?
835. In which round did Junior Witter stop opponent Giuseppe Lauri on 23 November 2002 – 2, 3 or 4?
836. At this stage of his career Junior Witter had now participated in how many professional contests – 26, 27 or 28?
837. Colin Lynes won the vacant IBO inter-continental light-welterweight title on 7 December 2002 when he stopped opponent Richard Kiley in which round – 9, 10 or 11?
838. Henry Akinwande won the WBN inter-continental heavyweight title on 10 December 2002 when he defeated opponent Roman Sukhoterin by which method - 4 round retirement, 6 round knockout or 12 round points decision?
839. On 14 December 2002 Ricky Hatton retained his WBU world light-welterweight title when he knocked out opponent Joe Hutchinson in which round – 3, 4 or 5?
840. Masamori Tokuyama retained his WBC super-flyweight title on 20 December 2002 when he defeated challenger Gerry Penalosa by which method - 1 round stoppage, 3 round retirement or 12 round points decision?

ROUND 85
NICKY COOK RETAINS COMMONWEALTH FEATHERWEIGHT TITLE

841. On 1 February 2003 Juan Manuel Márquez won the vacant IBF world featherweight title when he stopped Manuel Medina in which round – 5, 6 or 7?
842. In which American city did the Márquez v. Medina contest take place - Las Vegas, New York or Boston?
843. On 15 February 2003 Rafael Márquez won the IBF world bantamweight title when he stopped defending champion Tim Austin in which round – 6, 7 or 8?
844. True or false: IBF world featherweight champion Juan Manuel Márquez is the older brother of IBF world bantamweight king Rafael Márquez?
845. During his professional career, in which country did former European, British and Commonwealth heavyweight champion Henry Cooper not box – Sweden, Germany or America?
846. Nicky Cook retained his Commonwealth featherweight title on 31 May 2003 when he knocked out challenger David Kiilu in which round – 1, 2 or 3?
847. Who was the referee of the Cook v. Kiilu contest - Mark Green, Terry O'Connor or John Keane?
848. At this stage of his career Nicky Cook was now undefeated in how many professional contests – 20, 21 or 22?
849. Jane Couch met opponent Lucia Rijker on 21 June 2003 in an eight round contest. What was the result - A points win for Rijker, A draw or A points win for Couch?
850. On 21 June 2003 Lennox Lewis retained his WBC and IBO world heavyweight titles when challenger Vitali Klitschko was stopped in which round – 6, 7 or 8?

ROUND 86
BERNARD HOPKINS CONTINUES TO RULE THE WORLD OF MIDDLEWEIGHTS

851. On 28 June 2003 Joe Calzaghe retained his WBO world super-middleweight title when he stopped challenger Byron Mitchell in which round – 1, 2 or 3?
852. Where did the Calzaghe v. Mitchell contest take place – Cardiff, Glasgow or Manchester?
853. At this stage of his career Joe Calzaghe was now undefeated in how many professional contests – 34, 35 or 36?
854. On 1 August 2003 David Haye knocked out opponent Greg Scott-Briggs in which round – 1, 2 or 3?
855. Junior Witter retained his Commonwealth light-welterweight title on 27 September 2003 when he stopped challenger Fred Kinuthia in which round – 1, 2 or 3?
856. Ricky Hatton retained his WBU world light-welterweight title on 27 September 2003 when challenger Aldi Rios retired in which round – 8, 9 or 10?
857. Bernard Hopkins retained his WBC, WBA and IBF world middleweight titles on 13 December 2003 when he defeated challenger William Joppy by which method - 3 round stoppage, 6 round knockout or 12 round points decision?
858. In which American city did the Hopkins v. Joppy contest take place - Atlantic City, Boston or Las Vegas?
859. Wayne Braithwaite retained his WBC world cruiserweight title on 13 December 2003 when he stopped challenger Luis Andres Pineda in which round – 1, 2 or 3?
860. How many contests did David Haye have during 2003 – 5, 6 or 7?

ROUND 87
CARL FROCH BECOMES KING OF COMMONWEALTH SUPER-MIDDLEWEIGHTS

861. Carl Froch won the Commonwealth super-middleweight title on 12 March 2004 when he defeated Charles Adamu by which method - 2 round retirement, 6 round stoppage or 12 round points decision?
862. Who was the referee of the Froch v. Adamu contest - Terry O'Connor, Dave Parris or Marcus McDonnell?
863. Carl Froch was now undefeated in how many contests – 10, 11 or 12?
864. On 20 March 2004 David Haye stopped opponent Hastings Rasani in the first round. How many times had Haye now won in the opening round – 2, 3 or 4?
865. During his professional career which heavyweight title did Frank Bruno not hold – British, European or World?
866. Colin Lynes won the IBO world light-welterweight title on 8 May 2004 when he defeated defending champion Pablo Sarmiento by which method - 5 round knock out, 8 round stoppage or 12 round points decision?
867. Antonio Tarver regained the WBC world light-heavyweight title on 15 May 2004 when he stopped defending champion Roy Jones Jr in which round – 1, 2 or 3?
868. On 2 June 2004 Junior Witter won the vacant European light-welterweight title when he stopped Salvatore Battaglia in which round - 2, 3 or 4?
869. In which country did former WBC world, European and British lightweight champion Jim Watt not box during his professional career – Nigeria, France or America?
870. Arturo Gatti retained his WBC world light-welterweight title on 24 July 2004 when he knocked out challenger Leonardo Dorin in which round – 1, 2 or 3?

ROUND 88
MIKKEL KESSLER WINS VACANT WBA WORLD SUPER-MIDDLEWEIGHT TITLE

871. Bernard Hopkins retained his WBC, WBA and IBF world middleweight titles on 18 September 2004 and also won the WBO crown from holder Oscar De La Hoya when he knocked him out in which round – 9, 10 or 11?
872. Jeff Lacy won the vacant IBF super-middleweight title on 2 October 2004 when he stopped opponent Syd Vanderpool in which round – 8, 9 or 10?
873. In which American city did the Lacy v. Vanderpool con test take place - Las Vegas, New York or Boston?
874. At this stage of his career Jeff Lacy was now undefeated in how many professional contests – 17, 18 or 19?
875. Mikkel Kessler won the WBA world super-middleweight title on 12 November 2004 when holder Manny Siaca retired in which round – 6, 7 or 8?
876. In which country did the Kessler v. Siaca contest take place – Australia, America or Denmark?
877. At this stage of his professional career Mikkel Kessler was now undefeated in how many professional contests – 33, 34 or 35?
878. On 13 November 2004 John Ruiz retained his WBA world heavyweight title when he defeated challenger Andrew Golota by which method - 6 round knockout, Draw or 12 round points decision?
879. In which American city did the Ruiz v. Golota contest take place - New York, Atlantic City or Las Vegas?
880. On 16 December 2004 Vic Darchinyan won the IBF world flyweight title when he stopped defending champion Irene Pacheco in round 11 in a contest in which country – Australia, America or France?

ROUND 89
RICKY HATTON CAPTURES IBF WORLD LIGHT-WELTERWEIGHT TITLE

881. On 19 February 2005 Junior Witter retained his Commonwealth light-welterweight title when he defeated challenger Lovemore N'dou by which method - 3 round stoppage, 6 round knockout or 12 round points decision?
882. In which country did the Witter v. N'dou contest take place – Australia, America or England?
883. Joe Calzaghe retained his WBO world super-middleweight title on 7 May 2005 when he stopped challenger Mario Veit in which round – 4, 5 or 6?
884. In which country did the Calzaghe v. Veit contest take place – Germany, Denmark or England?
885. At this stage of his career Joe Calzaghe was now undefeated in how many professional contests – 37, 38 or 39?
886. Ricky Hatton won the IBF world light-welterweight title on 4 June 2005 when he stopped defending champion Kostya Tszyu in which round – 10, 11 or 12?
887. At this stage of his career Ricky Hatton was now undefeated in how many professional contests – 39, 40 or 41?
888. Mikkel Kessler retained his WBA world super-middleweight title on 8 June 2005 when he defeated challenger Anthony Mundine by which method - 6 round retirement, 8 round knockout or 12 round points decision?
889. In which country did the Kessler v. Mundine contest take place – Denmark, Australia or America?
890. Esham Pickering retained his European super-bantamweight title on 9 June 2005 when he stopped challenger Miguel Mallon in which round – 9, 10 or 11?

ROUND 90
JERMAIN TAYLOR WINS WORLD MIDDLEWEIGHT TITLES

891. In which country did the Esham Pickering v. Miguel Mallon contest take place – England, Italy or Spain?
892. Floyd Mayweather Jr. won the WBC world light-welterweight title on the 25 June 2005 when holder Arturo Gatti retired in which round - 6, 7 or 8?
893. Jermain Taylor won the WBC, WBA, IBF and WBO world middleweight titles on 16 July 2005 when he defeated defending champion Bernard Hopkins by which method - 3 round stoppage, 8 round knockout or 12 round points decision?
894. Jeff Lacy retained his IBF world super-middleweight title and won the IBO crown from Robin Reid on 6 August 2005 by which method - 3 round knockout, 8 round retirement or 12 round points decision?
895. Which version of the world super-middleweight title did Robin Reid previously hold – WBA, WBC or IBF?
896. On 24 August 2005 Vic Darchinyan retained his IBF world flyweight title when he stopped challenger Jair Jiménez in which round – 4, 5 or 6?
897. In which country did the Darchinyan v. Jiménez contest take place – Australia, America or Belgium?
898. Ross Minter retained his Southern Area welterweight title on 23 September 2005 when he stopped challenger Sammy Smith in which round – 1, 2 or 3?
899. True or false: Ross Minter is the son of former world middleweight champion Alan Minter?
900. Jermain Taylor retained his WBC, WBA, IBF and WBO world middleweight titles on 3 December 2005 against challenger Bernard Hopkins by which method - 4 round retirement, Draw or 12 round points decision?

ROUND 91
RICKY HATTON WINS WBA WORLD WELTERWEIGHT TITLE

901. On 26 November 2005 Ricky Hatton defended his IBF world light-welterweight title, challenging holder Carlos Maussa for the WBA version of the championship, and won by a knockout in which round – 9, 10 or 11?
902. On 4 March 2006 Joe Calzaghe defended his world WBO super-middleweight title, challenging holder Jeff Lacy for the IBF version of the championship, and won by which method - 2 round stoppage, 6 round knock out or 12 round points decision?
903. At this stage of his career Joe Calzaghe was now undefeated in how many professional contests – 40, 41 or 42?
904. David Haye retained his European cruiserweight title on 24 March 2006 when he stopped challenger Lasse Johansen in which round – 6, 7 or 8?
905. Clinton Woods retained his IBF world light-heavy weight title on 13 May 2006 when he stopped challenger Jason DeLisle in which round – 4, 5 or 6?
906. Ricky Hatton challenged Luis Collazo for the WBA world welterweight title on 13 May 2006 and won by which method - 6 round stoppage, 8 round knockout or 12 round points decision?
907. In which American city did the Hatton v. Collazo contest take place – Boston, New or Las Vegas?
908. How many times had Ricky Hatton now fought in America during his time in the professional ranks – 2, 3 or 4?
909. On 20 May 2006 Amir Khan outpointed opponent Laszlo Komjathi over how many rounds – 4, 6 or 8?
910. Miguel Cotto retained his WBO world light-welter weight title on 10 June 2006 when he defeated challenger Paulie Malignaggi by which method - 4 round retirement, 6 round knockout or 12 round points decision?

ROUND 92
JUNIOR WITTER WINS VACANT WBC WORLD LIGHT-WELTERWEIGHT CROWN

911. During his professional career in which weight division was Toro George a Commonwealth champion – Bantamweight, Featherweight or Lightweight?
912. During his professional career which European title did Tom Bogs not hold – Middleweight, Light-heavyweight or Heavyweight?
913. Scott Gammer won the vacant British heavyweight title on 16 June 2006 when he stopped opponent Mark Krence in which round – 7, 8 or 9?
914. Where did the Gammer v. Krence contest take place – Carmarthen, Aberavon or Newport?
915. On 15 September 2006 Junior Witter won the vacant WBC world light-welterweight title when he defeated DeMarcus Corley by which method - 9 round stoppage, 10 round retirement or 12 round points decision?
916. In how many professional contests had Junior Witter now participated – 36, 37 or 38?
917. On 24 September 2006 Cathy Brown won the vacant women's English bantamweight title when she defeated opponent Juliette Winter by which method - 6 round stoppage, 8 round knockout or 10 round points decision?
918. Amir Khan won the vacant IBF inter-continental light-welterweight title on 9 December 2006 when he defeated Rachid Drilzane by which method - 1 round stoppage, 6 round knockout or 10 round points decision?
919. At this stage of his career Amir Khan was now undefeated in how many professional contests – 10, 11 or 12?
920. How many times did Jane Couch box in the year 2006 – 1, 2 or 3?

ROUND 93
FLOYD MAYWEATHER JR DEFEATS OSCAR DE LA HOYA

921. On 20 January 2007 Ricky Hatton regained his IBF world light-welterweight title and won the vacant IBO crown when he defeated defending champion Juan Urango by which method - 3 round knockout, 9 round retirement or 12 round points decision?
922. In which American city did the Hatton v. Urango contest take place - Las Vegas, New York or Boston?
923. Ricky Hatton was now undefeated in how many professional contests – 42, 43 or 44?
924. Kevin Mitchell retained his Commonwealth super-featherweight title on 10 March 2007 when he stopped challenger Harry Ramogoadi in which round – 5, 6 or 7?
925. Who was the referee of the Mitchell v. Ramogoadi contest - Phil Edwards, Marcus McDonnell or Howard Foster?
926. Floyd Mayweather Jr won the WBC world light-middleweight title on 5 May 2007 when he defeated defending champion Oscar De La Hoya by which method - 6 round stoppage, 9 round retirement or 12 round points decision?
927. At this stage of his career Floyd Mayweather Jr was now undefeated in how many professional contests – 37, 38 or 39?
928. Colin Lynes won the British light-welterweight title on 8 June 2007 when he defeated defending champion Barry Morrison by which method - 4 round knockout, 7 round retirement or 12 round points decision?
929. Who was the referee of the Lynes v. Morrison contest - Mark Green, Phil Edwards or Victor Loughlin?
930. Miguel Cotto retained his WBA world welterweight title on 9 June 2007 when he stopped challenger Zab Judah in which round – 9, 10 or 11?

ROUND 94
PAULIE MALIGNAGGI WINS IBF LIGHT-WELTERWEIGHT CROWN

931. Miguel Cotto was now undefeated in how many professional contests – 29, 30 or 31?
932. Paulie Malignaggi won the IBF world light-welter weight title on 16 June 2007 when he defeated defending champion Lovemore N'dou by which method - 1 round stoppage, 6 round knockout or 12 round points decision?
933. In which year was Paulie Malignaggi born – 1980, 1981 or 1982?
934. True or false: Jane Couch lost a 10 round points decision on 20 June 2007 for the vacant world IBF light-welterweight title?
935. Ricky Hatton retained his IBO world light-welter weight title on 23 June 2007 and won the vacant WBC international light-welterweight crown when he knocked out challenger José Luis Castillio in which round – 3, 4 or 5?
936. In which country did the Hatton v. Castillio contest take place – America, England or Canada?
937. On 23 June 2007 Matthew Hatton defended his IBF inter-continental welterweight title when he defeated challenger Edwin Vázquez by which method - 2 round knockout, 8 round retirement or 12 round points decision?
938. Felix Sturm retained his WBA world middleweight crown on 30 June 2007 when he defeated challenger Noé Tulio González by which method - 3 round stop page, Draw or 12 round points decision?
939. In which German city did the Sturm v. González contest take place – Hamburg, Stuttgart or Berlin?
940. In which weight division was Joe Bygraves a Commonwealth champion (then Empire) in the professional ranks – Middleweight, Light-heavyweight or Heavyweight?

ROUND 95
COLIN LYNES IS NEW EUROPEAN LIGHT-WELTERWEIGHT KING

941. Leva Kirakosyan retained his European super-feather weight title on 13 July 2007 when he knocked out challenger Carl Johanneson in which round – 3, 4 or 5?
942. On 14 July 2007 Steve Luevano won the vacant WBO world featherweight title when he knocked out opponent Nicky Cook in which round – 10, 11 or 12?
943. Amir Khan won the Commonwealth lightweight title on 14 July 2007 when defending champion Willie Limond retired in which round – 8, 9 or 10?
944. Colin Lynes retained his British light-welterweight title on 20 July 2007 and also won the vacant European light-welterweight title when he stopped Young Muttley in which round – 7, 8 or 9?
945. Who was the European light-welterweight champion prior to Colin Lynes - Junior Witter, Ted Bami or Oktay Urkal?
946. In which weight division was Young Muttley a former British champion prior to his contest with Colin Lynes – Lightweight, Light-welterweight or Welterweight?
947. Enzo Maccarinelli retained his WBO world cruiser weight title on 21 July 2007 when he defeated challenger Wayne Braithwaite by which method - 6 round stoppage, 9 round knockout or 12 round points decision?
948. Who held the WBO world cruiserweight title prior to Enzo Maccarinelli - Johnny Nelson, Carl Thompson or Ralf Rocchigiani?
949. Souleymane M'baye lost his WBA world light-welter weight title on 21 July 2007 when Gavin Rees defeated him by which method - 2 round stoppage, 8 round retirement or 12 round points decision?
950. Which European title did Pat Cowdell not hold while boxing in the professional ranks – Featherweight, Super-featherweight or Lightweight?

ROUND 96
CALZAGHE DEFEATS KESSLER

951. What is the nationality of former WBC world light-heavyweight champion Jeff Harding – American, Australian or Canadian?
952. On 25 August 2007 Tony Oakey retained his British light-heavyweight title against challenger Brian Magee by which method - 1 round knockout, Draw or 12 round points decision?
953. Joe Calzaghe retained his WBO world super-middleweight title on 3 November 2007 and also won the WBC and WBA versions from the champion Mikkel Kessler when he defeated him by which method - 4 round stoppage, 6 round retirement or 12 round points decision?
954. Who was the referee of the Calzaghe v. Kessler contest - Mike Ortega, Frank Garza or Takeshi Shimakawa?
955. Prior to the contest with Joe Calzaghe Mikkel Kessler was undefeated in how many professional contests – 38, 39 or 40?
956. After his contest with Mikkel Kessler Joe Calzaghe was now undefeated in how many professional contests – 42, 43 or 44?
957. Which of the following boxers did Billy Walker not fight twice in the professional ranks - Brian London, Johnny Prescott or Eduardo Corletti?
958. Which version of the world cruiserweight title did Glenn McCrory hold in the professional ranks – WBC, WBA or IBF?
959. Former British champions Gary De'Roux (featherweight), John Doherty (super-featherweight) and Alex Dickson (lightweight) were all born in which year – 1961, 1962 or 1963?
960. True or false: former world WBO middleweight and super-middleweight champion Chris Eubank had his first five professional contests in America?

ROUND 97
DAVID HAYE KING OF THE CRUISERWEIGHT DIVISION

961. David Haye won the WBC and WBA world cruiser weight titles on 10 November 2007 when he stopped defending champion Jean-Marc Mormeck in which round – 5, 6 or 7?
962. In which country did the Haye v. Mormeck contest take place – America, France or England?
963. In which round was Haye floored for a count by Mormeck – 4, 5 or 6?
964. Who was the referee of the Haye v. Mormeck contest - Steve Smoger, Guido Cavalieri or Benji Esteves?
965. Amir Khan retained his Commonwealth lightweight title on 8 December 2007 when he stopped challenger Graham Earl in which round – 1, 2 or 3?
966. Who was the referee of the Khan v. Earl contest - Marcus McDonnell, Howard Foster or Wynford Jones?
967. On 8 December 2007 Brahim Asloum won the WBA world light-flyweight title when he defeated defending champion Juan Carlos Reveco by which method - 6 round stoppage, 8 round knockout or 12 round points decision?
968. Chris Edwards became the first man to hold the British super-flyweight title on 8 December 2007 when in the inaugural contest he defeated Jamie McDonnell by which method - 3 round stoppage, 8 round knockout or 12 round points decision?
969. Floyd Mayweather Jr retained his WBC world welter weight title on 8 December 2007 when he stopped challenger Ricky Hatton in which round – 9, 10 or 11?
970. Who was the referee of the Mayweather Jr v. Hatton contest - Joe Cortez, Tony Weeks or Kenny Bayless?

ROUND 98
TARVER DEFEATS WOODS
TO REGAIN IBF WORLD LIGHT-HEAVYWEIGHT CROWN

971. In which city did the Mayweather Jr v. Hatton world title contest take place - New York, Atlantic City or Las Vegas?
972. Danny Green won the WBA world light-heavyweight title on 16 December 2007 when he defeated defending champion Stipe Drews by which method - 2 round retirement, 6 round knockout or 12 round points decision?
973. Paulie Malignaggi retained his IBF world light-welterweight title on 5 January 2008 when he outpointed challengerHerman Ngoudjo over 12 rounds in a contest in which American city - Atlantic City, New York or San Francisco?
974. Colin Lynes retained his European light-welterweight title on 25 January 2008 when he defeated challenger Juho Tolppola by which method - 3 round knockout, Draw or 12 round points decision?
975. Amir Khan retained his Commonwealth lightweight title on 2 February 2008 when he defeated challenger Gairy St Clair by which method - 4 round knockout, 8 round stoppage or 12 round points decision?
976. In which weight division was Gairy St Clair once an IBF world champion – Featherweight, Super-featherweight or Lightweight?
977. On 8 March 2008 David Haye retained his WBC and WBA versions of the world cruiserweight title and won the WBO version of the championship from holder Enzo Maccarinelli, stopping him in which round – 1, 2 or 3?
978. Andreas Kotelnik won the WBA world light-welterweight title on 22 March 2008 when he stopped defending champion Gavin Rees in which round – 10, 11 or 12?
979. Antonio Tarver regained the IBF world light-heavyweight title in 2008 when he defeated defending champion Clinton Woods by which method - 6 round stoppage, 8 round knockout or 12 round points decision?
980. In which country did the Tarver v. Woods contest take place – Canada, America or England?

ROUND 99
JOE CALZAGHE DEFEATS BERNARD HOPKINS IN AMERICA

981. Joe Calzaghe defeated Bernard Hopkins by which method on 19 April 2008 - 5 round stoppage, 6 round knockout or 12 round points decision?

982. In which round did Hopkins floor Calzaghe for a count – 1, 2 or 3?

983. Who was the referee of the Calzaghe v. Hopkins contest - Dale Frye, Joe Cortez or Eddie Cotton?

984. In which American city did the Calzaghe v. Hopkins contest take place - New York, Las Vegas or Atlantic City?

985. True or false: this was Joe Calzaghe's first professional contest in America?

986. Timothy Bradley won the WBC world light-welterweight title on 10 May 2008, defeating champion Junior Witter by which method - 6 round retirement, 9 round stoppage or 12 round points decision?

987. On 16 May 2008 Gianluca Branco regained the European light-welterweight title when he defeated defending champion Colin Lynes by which method - 6 round retirement, 8 round knockout or 12 round points decision?

988. In which country did the Branco v. Lynes contest take place – Italy, Spain or England?

989. Craig Watson retained his Commonwealth welterweight title on 24 May 2008 when he defeated challenger Matthew Hatton by which method - 4 round retirement, Draw or 12 round points decision?

990. True or false: Craig Watson boxes in the southpaw stance?

ROUND 100
KESSLER REGAINS WBA WORLD SUPER-MIDDLEWEIGHT CROWN

991. Paulie Malignaggi retained his IBF world light-welter weight title on 24 May 2008 when he defeated challenger Lovemore N'dou by which method - 2 round stoppage, 6 round knockout or 12 round points decision?
992. Ricky Hatton defended which version of the world light-welterweight title on the 24 May 2008 - WBO, WBA or IBO?
993. Edwin Valero retained his WBA world super-feather weight title on 12 June 2008 when he defeated challenger Takehiro Shimada by which method - 4 round retirement, 7 round stoppage or 12 round points decision?
994. Valero was now undefeated in how many professional contests - 23, 24 or 25?
995. Amir Khan retained his Commonwealth lightweight title on 21 June 2008 when he stopped challenger Michael Gomez in which round – 3, 4 or 5?
996. On 21 June 2008 Mikkel Kessler regained the vacant WBA world super-middleweight title when he defeated opponent Dmitri Sartison by which method - 3 round retirement, 12 round stoppage or 12 round points decision?
997. In which country did the Kessler v. Sartison contest take place – Denmark, Germany or America?
998. Jamie Moore won the Irish light-middleweight title on 5 July 2008 when he stopped defending champion Ciaran Healey in which round – 1, 2 or 3?
999. True or False: Jamie Moore was a former British light-middleweight champion?
1000. Wladimir Klitschko retained his IBF, WBO and IBO world heavyweight titles on 12 July 2008 when he knocked out challenger Tony Thompson in which round – 10, 11 or 12?

ROUND 101
COTTO MEETS WITH DEFEAT

1001. On 18 July 2008 Danny Williams retained his British heavyweight title against challenger John McDermott by which method - 3 round stoppage, 6 round knock out or 12 round points decision?

1002. Who was the referee of the Williams v. McDermott contest - Dave Parris, Jeff Hinds or Wynford Jones?

1003. John McDermott had previously challenged for the British heavyweight title on 10 December 2005 when the then reigning champion Matt Skelton stopped him in which round – 1, 2 or 3?

1004. Who was the referee of the Skelton v. McDermott contest - Mickey Vann, Terry O'Connor or John Keane?

1005. On 23 July 2008 Jeff Lacy outpointed opponent Epifanio Mendoza over how many rounds – 8, 10 or 12?

1006. Who was the referee of the Lacy v. Mendoza contest - Jack Reiss, Tony Weeks or Toby Gibson?

1007. Antonio Margarito won the WBA world welterweight title on 26 July 2008 when he stopped defending champion Miguel Cotto in which round – 9, 10 or 11?

1008. Who was the referee of the Margarito v. Cotto contest - Kenny Bayless, Jay Nady or Robert Byrd?

1009. In which American city did the Margarito v. Cotto contest take place - New York, Las Vegas or Atlantic City?

1010. Prior to his defeat to Margarito Cotto was undefeated in how many professional contests – 30, 31 or 32?

ROUND 102
ANTHONY MUNDINE DEFEATS CRAZY KIM

1011. Glen Hamada and Dave Moretti were two of the ring side judges during the Margarito v. Cotto world title contest, but who was the third - Jerry Roth, Duane Ford or Ricardo Ocasio?
1012. What is the nationality of Antonio Margarito – French, Mexican or American?
1013. What is the nationality of Miguel Cotto – Mexican, Spanish or Puerto Rican?
1014. During his professional career Sid Smith held a world title in which weight division – Flyweight, Bantamweight or Featherweight?
1015. In which year was former British, European and Commonwealth welterweight champion Gary Jacobs born – 1963, 1964 or 1965?
1016. On 30 July 2008 José Luis Castillo and Sebastian Lujan met in a 10 round contest. What was the result – Draw, Points win for Castillio or Points win for Lujan?
1017. In which weight division was Castillio a two-times WBC world title holder – Lightweight, Light-welterweight or Welterweight?
1018. On 30 July 2008 former WBA world super-middleweight champion Anthony Mundine defeated opponent Crazy Kim by which method - 4 round stoppage, 6 round knockout or 10 round points decision?
1019. In which country did the Mundine v. Kim contest take place – Japan, Australia or America?
1020. Billy Dib won the vacant IBO world super-feather weight title on 30 July 2008 when he defeated opponent Zolani Marali by which method - 4 round retirement, 6 round stoppage or 12 round points decision?

ROUND 103
NAITO RETAINS WBC WORLD FLYWEIGHT CROWN

1021. During his professional career which heavyweight title did Horace Notice not hold – British, Commonwealth or European?
1022. Daisuke Naito retained his WBC world flyweight title on 30 July 2008 when he knocked out challenger Tomonobu Shimizu in which round – 10, 11 or 12?
1023. Who was the referee of the Naito v. Shimizu contest - Robert Ferrara, Frank Garza or Kazunobu Asao?
1024. In which country did the Naito v. Shimizu contest take place – Japan, Australia or America?
1025. Takefumi Sakata retained his WBA world flyweight title on 30 July 2008 when he defeated challenger Hiroyuki Hisataka by which method - 1 round stoppage, 6 round knockout or 12 round points decision?
1026. Vic Darchinyan won the IBF world super-flyweight title on 2 August 2008 when he knocked out defending champion Dimitri Kirilov in which round – 5, 6 or 7?
1027. Who was the referee of the Darchinyan v. Kirilov contest - Earl Brown, Joe Cortez or Johnny Callas?
1028. In which country did the Darchinyan v. Kirilov contest take place – Australia, France or America?
1029. Which boxer was not managed by Terry Lawless during his respective professional career - Frank Bruno, Jim Watt or Howard Winstone?
1030. In which year did Joe Calzaghe win the ABA welter weight title – 1991, 1992 or 1993?

ROUND 104
JOSHUA CLOTTEY WINS VACANT IBF WORLD WELTERWEIGHT CROWN

1031. When Ricky Hatton enters the ring to box, he does so with which song being played - 'Magic Moments', 'Blue Moon' or 'Moon River'?
1032. In the 2004 Olympic Games Amir Khan won which medal in the lightweight division – Bronze, Silver or Gold?
1033. Which version of the world light-middleweight title did Mike McCallum formerly hold – WBC, IBF or WBA?
1034. Which opponent did Randy Turpin not meet during his professional career - Rocky Graziano, Carl Olson or Don Cockell?
1035. Which boxer was not managed by Terry Lawless during his professional career - Maurice Hope, Charlie Magri or Alan Minter?
1036. Which version of the world middleweight title did Otis Grant formerly hold – WBC, WBA or WBO
1037. Joshua Clottey won the vacant IBF world welterweight title on 2 August 2008 when he defeated opponent Zab Judah on a technical points decision, the contest terminating in which round – 7, 8 or 9?
1038. Who was the referee of the Clottey v. Judah contest - Robert Byrd, Robert Ferrara or Malik Waleed?
1039. In which American city did the Clottey v. Judah contest take place - Atlantic City, New York or Las Vegas?
1040. What is the nationality of Joshua Clottey – American, Ghanaian or French?

ROUND 105
JAMES DEGALE WINS OLYMPIC GOLD MEDAL

1041. On 11 August 2008 Ann Marie Saccurato defeated opponent Fujin Raika by which method to win the vacant WBC world lightweight title - 3 round stoppage, 6 round knockout or 10 round points decision?
1042. Who was the referee of the Saccurato v. Raika contest - Gene Del Branco, Robert Byrd or Geno Rodríguez?
1043. In which country did the Saccurato v. Raika contest take place – America, Thailand or Japan?
1044. On 15 August 2008 Darren Barker outpointed opponent Larry Sharpe over how many rounds – 8, 10 or 12?
1045. At the time of the Barker v. Sharpe contest which title did Barker hold – British, European or Commonwealth?
1046. In which country did the Barker v. Sharpe contest take place – Canada, America or Germany?
1047. In the 2008 Olympic Games held in China Britain's James DeGale won a gold medal in which weight division – Welterweight, Middleweight or Light-heavyweight?
1048. To win his gold medal James DeGale outpointed opponent Emilio Correa over four rounds. What is Correa's nationality – Cuban, Mexican or American?
1049. Which boxer did former British light-middleweight champion Larry Paul not box during his professional career - Alan Minter, Rocky Mattioli or Marvin Hagler?
1050. Which version of the world middleweight title did Jason Matthews formerly hold – WBO, WBC or IBF?

ROUND 106
MIJARES RETAINS WORLD WBC AND WBA SUPER-FLYWEIGHT TITLES

1051. Susianna Kentikian retained her WBA and WIBF world flyweight titles on 29 August 2008 when she defeated challenger Hagar Shmoulefeld-Finer by which method – 2 round retirement, 5 round knockout or 10 round points decision?
1052. In which country did the Kentikian v. Shmoulefeld-Finer contest take place – Finland, Poland or Germany?
1053. Steve Molitor retained his IBF world super-bantamweight title on 29 August 2008 when he stopped challenger Ceferino Dario Labarda in which round – 9, 10 or 11?
1054. Who was the referee of the Molitor v. Labarda contest – Charlie Fitch, Steve Smoger or Tony Weeks?
1055. In which country did the Molitor v. Labarda contest take place – America, Canada or Mexico?
1056. Donnie Nietes retained his WBO world strawweight title on 30 August 2008, stopping challenger Eddy Castro in which round – 2, 3 or 4?
1057. Who was the referee of the Nietes v. Castro contest - Raúl Caiz Jr, Earl Brown or Tony Crebs?
1058. On 30 August 2008 Cristian Mijares retained his WBC and WBA world super-flyweight titles when he stopped challenger Chatchai Sasakul in which round – 2, 3 or 4?
1059. Who was the referee of the Mijares v. Sasakul contest - Toby Gibson, Mickey Vann or Andrew Smale?
1060. In which country did the Mijares v. Sasakul contest take place – America, South Africa or Mexico?

ROUND 107
TALLEST MAN TO HOLD A VERSION OF THE WORLD HEAVYWEIGHT TITLE

1061. Nikolai Valuev regained the WBA world heavyweight title when he defeated John Ruiz for the vacant crown on 30 August 2008 by which method - 5 round retirement, 6 round stoppage or 12 round points decision?
1062. In which country did the Valuev v. Ruiz contest take place – America, Germany or France?
1063. Who was the referee of the Valuev v. Ruiz contest - Terry O'Connor, Derek Milham or Tony Weeks?
1064. Nikolai Valuev is the tallest man to hold a version of the world heavyweight title. What is his listed height - 6 foot, 6 inches, 6 foot, 9 inches or 7 foot?
1065. During his professional career which opponent did former Welsh heavyweight champion Carl Gizzi not box - Billy Walker, Billy Wynter or Billy Gray?
1066. On 30 August 2008 Lamon Brewster knocked out opponent Danny Batchelder in which round – 4, 5 or 6?
1067. Which version of the world heavyweight title did Lamon Brewster formerly hold – WBO, WBA or WBC?
1068. 1998 was Ricky Hatton's most active year. How many times did he box during that period – 7, 8 or 9?
1069. True or false: Ricky Hatton held the European light-welterweight title before becoming a world champion in that division?
1070. Which of the following former world heavyweight champions did not box in Britain during their professional career - Rocky Marciano, Joe Frazier or Floyd Patterson?

ROUND 108
MUNROE RETAINS EUROPEAN SUPER-BANTAMWEIGHT TITLE

1071. On 5 September 2008 Alfred Cole outpointed opponent Joey Abel over how many rounds – 6, 8 or 10?

1072. In which country did the Cole v. Abel contest take place – America, Denmark or Sweden?

1073. Which version of the world cruiserweight title did Alfred Cole formerly hold – WBA, IBF or WBC?

1074. On 5 September 2008 Kevin Johnson knocked out opponent Bruce Seldon in which round – 4, 5 or 6?

1075. Which version of the world heavyweight title did Bruce Seldon formerly hold – WBA, WBC or IBF?

1076. In which American city did the Johnson v. Seldon contest take place - Las Vegas, Atlantic City or New York?

1077. True or false: Bruce Seldon once fought Frank Bruno in the professional ranks?

1078. Rendall Munroe retained his European super-bantamweight title on 5 September 2008 when he defeated challenger Arsen Martirosian by which method - 3 round stoppage, 8 round knockout or 12 round points decision?

1079. Where did the Munroe v. Martirosian contest take place – Nottingham, Manchester or London?

1080. Oleg Maskaev outpointed opponent Robert Hawkins over how many rounds on 6 September 2008 – 8, 10 or 12?

ROUND 109
NICKY COOK WINS WBO WORLD SUPER-FEATHERWEIGHT TITLE

1081. In which country did the Oleg Maskaev v. Robert Hawkins contest take place – America, Russia or France?

1082. Which version of the world heavyweight title did Oleg Maskaev formerly hold – WBC, WBA or IBF?

1083. True or false: Carl Froch won the ABA middleweight title twice?

1084. On 6 September 2008 Nicky Cook won the WBO world super-featherweight title when he defeated defending champion Alex Arthur by which method - 3 round stoppage, 9 round knockout or 12 round points decision?

1085. Who was the referee of the Cook v. Arthur contest - Mickey Vann, John Keane or Mark Green?

1086. In which weight division did Nicky Cook formerly hold a European title – Bantamweight, Super-bantamweight or Featherweight?

1087. Where did the Cook v. Arthur contest take place – Liverpool, Manchester or Birmingham?

1088. Audley Harrison defeated opponent George Arias by which method on 6 September 2008 - 3 round stoppage, 6 round knockout or 10 round points decision?

1089. True or false: Audley Harrison boxes in the southpaw stance?

1090. In which weight division did Audley Harrison win a gold medal in the 2000 Olympic Games in Sydney, Australia - Light-heavyweight, Heavyweight or Super-heavyweight?

ROUND 110
AMIR KHAN'S FIRST DEFEAT IN THE PROFESSIONAL RANKS

1091. Breidis Prescott won the WBO inter-continental lightweight title on 6 September 2008 when he knocked out Amir Khan in which round – 1, 2 or 3?

1092. Going into the contest against Khan Prescott was underfeated in how many professional contests – 17, 18 or 19?

1093. Going into the contest against Prescott Khan was undefeated in how many professional contests – 17, 18 or 19?

1094. How old was Khan at the time of the Prescott contest – 20, 21 or 22?

1095. How old was Prescott at the time of the Khan contest – 23, 24 or 25?

1096. What is the nationality of Prescott – American, French or Colombian?

1097. Who was the referee of the Khan v. Prescott contest - Terry O'Connor, Jeff Hinds or Richie Davies?

1098. True or false: the contest against Khan was the first time that Prescott had fought in Britain?

1099. Who was the British lightweight champion at the time of the Khan v. Prescott contest - John Murray, Jonathan Thaxton or Lee Meager?

1100. True or false: prior to the Prescott contest Khan had boxed twice in America during his time in the professional ranks?

ROUND 111
SMALL WINS TITLE

1101. The film Raging Bull was based on which former world middleweight champion - Jake LaMotta, Rocky Graziano or Tony Zale?

1102. In which year was Joe Louis elected into the Boxing Hall of Fame – 1953, 1954 or 1955?

1103. On 12 September 2008 Anthony Small won the vacant WBA international light-middleweight title when he stopped opponent Freddy Curiel in which round – 9, 10 or 11?

1104. Who was the referee of the Small v. Curiel contest - Terry O'Connor, John Keane or Jeff Hinds?

1105. Where did the Small v. Curiel contest take place – Manchester, Liverpool or London?

1106. Who was the British light-middleweight champion at the time of the Small v. Curiel contest - Ryan Rhodes, Gary Woolcombe or Jamie Moore?

1107. In which round during a heavyweight contest on 12 September 2008 did Derek Chisora stop opponent Shawn McClean – 5, 6 or 7?

1108. In which weight division did Derek Chisora win an ABA title in 2006 - Light-heavyweight, Heavyweight or Super-heavyweight?

1109. Who is reputed to have said before a defence of the world heavyweight title: "He can run but he can't hide" - Rocky Marciano, Joe Louis or Floyd Patterson?

1110. The film The Hurricane was based on which former world middleweight challenger - Bennie Briscoe, Rubin Carter or Tom Bethea?

ROUND 112
VERNON FORREST REGAINS WBC WORLD LIGHT-MIDDLEWEIGHT CROWN

1111. In the 1998 Commonwealth Games in Malaysia Audley Harrison won a gold medal in which weight division - Light-heavyweight, Heavyweight or Super-heavy weight?

1112. Juan Manuel Márquez stopped opponent Joel Casamayor in which round on 13 September 2008 – 10, 11 or 12?

1113. Who was the referee of the Márquez v. Casamayor contest - Tony Weeks, Alexander Kalinkin or Joe Cortez?

1114. Vernon Forrest regained the WBC world light-middleweight title on 13 September 2008 when he defeated defending champion Sergio Mora by which method - 6 round stoppage, 8 round knockout or 12 round points decision?

1115. How old was Vernon Forrest at the time of the contest – 36, 37 or 38?

1116. What is Forrest's nickname - The Viper, The Sniper or The Wiper?

1117. Who was the referee of the Forrest v. Mora contest - Vic Drakulich, Luis Pabón or Roberto Ramírez Jr?

1118. In which American city did the Forrest v. Mora contest take place - Atlantic City, Boston or Las Vegas?

1119. True or false: Vernon Forrest was a former holder of the WBC and IBF world welterweight title?

1120. In which year was Floyd Patterson elected into The Boxing Hall of Fame – 1976, 1977 or 1978?

ROUND 113
KOTELNIK RETAINS WBA WORLD LIGHT-WELTERWEIGHT CHAMPIONSHIP

1121. Which boxer had a left hook nicknamed 'Enry's 'Ammer - Henry Armstrong, Henry Cooper or Henry Akinwande?

1122. On 13 September 2008 Raúl Garcia retained his IBF world strawweight title against challenger José Luis Varela by which method - 3 round retirement, 6 round knockout or 12 round points decision?

1123. Who was the referee of the Garcia v. Varela contest - Terry O'Connor, Jack Reiss or Mark Nelson?

1124. What is the nationality of Raúl Garcia – Spanish, Mexican or American?

1125. What is the nationality of José Luis Varela – Cuban, Venezuelan or Colombian?

1126. Andreas Kotelnik retained his WBA world light-welterweight title on 13 September 2008 when he defeated challenger Norio Kimura by which method - 1 round stoppage, 6 round knockout or 12 round points decision?

1127. What is the nationality of Andreas Kotelnik – Russian, Polish or Ukrainian?

1128. What is the nationality of Norio Kimura – American, Japanese or Australian?

1129. Who was the referee of the Kotelnik v. Kimura contest - Stanley Christodoulou, Kenny Bayless or Benjy Esteves?

1130. Who was the British light-welterweight champion at the time of the Kotelnik v. Kimura contest - Colin Lynes, David Barnes or Barry Morrison?

ROUND 114
BRADLEY RETAINS WBC WORLD LIGHT-WELTERWEIGHT TITLE

1131. Timothy Bradley retained his WBC world light-welterweight title on 13 September 2008 when he defeated challenger Edner Cherry by which method - 8 round stoppage, 11 round knockout or 12 round points decision?

1132. What is Timothy Bradley's nickname - Desert Storm, Rain Storm or Snow Storm?

1133. At this stage of his career Bradley was now undefeated in how many professional contests – 21, 22 or 23?

1134. How old was Bradley at the time of the Cherry contest – 24, 25 or 26?

1135. In which country did the Bradley v. Cherry contest take place – Canada, Australia or America?

1136. Who held the Commonwealth light-welterweight title at the time of the Bradley v. Cherry contest - Ajose Olusegun, Junior Witter or Lenny Dawes?

1137. Cathy Brown's most active year in the ring was during 2001. How many times did she box during that time – 3, 4 or 5?

1138. In which year was Rocky Graziano elected to the Boxing Hall of Fame – 1971, 1972 or 1973?

1139. How many times did Sugar Ray Robinson box in Scotland during his professional career (not including exhibition bouts) – 1, 2 or 3?

1140. In the film Ali, based on the life story of Muhammad Ali, which actor played the title role - Denzel Washington, Will Smith or Jamie Foxx?

ROUND 115
BALOYI RETAINS HIS IBF WORLD SUPER-FEATHERWEIGHT TITLE

1141. On 13 September 2008 Cassius Baloyi retained his IBF world super-featherweight title by stopping challenger Javier Álvarez in which round – 1, 2 or 3?

1142. How old was Baloyi at the time of the Álvarez contest – 32, 33 or 34?

1143. What is the nationality of Álvarez – Argentinian, Mexican or Spanish?

1144. What is the nationality of Baloyi - South African, Australian or American?

1145. True or false: Nick Durandt was Baloyi's manager?

1146. True or false: Kevin Mitchell was the holder of the British and Commonwealth super-featherweight titles at the time of the Baloyi v. Álvarez contest?

1147. Who was the referee of the Baloyi v. Álvarez contest - William Sikeleti, Sparkle Lee or John Keane?

1148. In which country did the Baloyi v. Álvarez contest take place - South Africa, America or Australia?

1149. Isaac Chilembe won the vacant African Boxing Union (ABU) super-middleweight title on 13 September 2008 when he defeated opponent Charles Adamu by which method - 1 round stoppage, 6 round knockout or 12 round points decision?

1150. True or false: at an early stage of his professional career Isaac Chilembe lost a 10 round points decision to Joe Calzaghe?

ROUND 116
JACKIEWICZ WINS EUROPEAN WELTERWEIGHT TITLE

1151. On 14 September 2008 Rafal Jackiewicz won the European welterweight title when he defeated defending champion Jackson Osei Bonsu by which method - 6 round knockout, 8 round stoppage or 12 round points decision?
1152. Franco Ciminale and Robert Verwijs were two of the judges at the Jackiewicz v. Bonsu contest, but who was the third - Mikael Hook, Mickey Vann or Roy Francis?
1153. At the time of the Jackiewicz v. Bonsu contest who was the WBO world welterweight champion - Daniel Santos, Ahmed Kotiev or Paul Williams?
1154. True or false: at an early stage of his professional career Rafal Jackiewicz was once defeated by Ricky Hatton by way of a 10 round points decision?
1155. At the time of the Jackiewicz v. Bonsu contest who was the British welterweight champion - Kell Brook, Kevin Anderson or Michael Jennings?
1156. Prior to the Jackiewicz v. Bonsu contest who was the last British boxer to hold the European welterweight title - Kirkland Laing, Gary Jacobs or Lloyd Honeyghan?
1157. On 14 September 2008 Lee Edwards won the vacant British Masters light-middleweight title when he defeated opponent Alex Matvienko by which method - 3 round stoppage, 7 round knockout or 10 round points decision?
1158. Who was the referee of the Edwards v. Matvienko contest - Steve Grey, Mark Green or Jeff Hinds?
1159. Where did the Edwards v. Matvienko contest take place – London, Wigan or Swansea?
1160. In which year did Edwards make his professional debut – 2003, 2004 or 2005?

ROUND 117
GONZÁLEZ WINS WBA WORLD STRAWWEIGHT TITLE

1161. Who was the first holder of the IBF world super-middleweight title - Murray Sutherland, Chong Pal Park or Graciano Rocchigiani?

1162. How many times did Arthur Donovan referee a Joe Louis world heavyweight title contest -10, 11 or 12?

1163. How many professional contests did former British and Empire middleweight champion Dick Turpin have during his professional career -101, 102 or 103?

1164. Who was the first boxer to regain the WBO world heavyweight title - Herbie Hide, Henry Akinwande or Tommy Morrison?

1165. True or false: during his professional career former British and Commonwealth middleweight champion Mark Rowe did not box in America?

1166. On 15 September 2008 Román 'Chocolate' González won the WBA world strawweight title when he defeated defending champion Yutaka Niida by which method - 3 round stoppage, 4 round stoppage or 6 round knockout?

1167. How old was González at the time of the Niida contest – 20, 21 or 22?

1168. How old was Niida at the time of the González contest – 29, 30 or 31?

1169. What is the nationality of González – American, Nicaraguan or Mexican?

1170. What is the nationality of Niida – Japanese, French or Canadian?

ROUND 118
SAME YEAR OF BIRTH

1171. True or false: Lennox Lewis once held the WBO world heavyweight title during his professional career?

1172. How many times did former world heavyweight champion Muhammad Ali box in New York during his professional career – 8, 9 or 10?

1173. Floyd Mayweather Jr, Colin Lynes and Pongsaklek Wonjongkam were all born in which year – 1976, 1977 or 1978?

1174. On 15 September 2008 Toshiaki Nishioka won the WBC interim super-bantamweight title when he defeated opponent Napapol Kiatisakchokchai by which method - 2 round retirement, 6 round knockout or 12 round points decision?

1175. Who was the referee of the Nishioka v. Kiatisakchokchai contest - Mark Green, Kenny Bayless or Alexander Kalinkin?

1176. True or false: Nishioka boxes in the southpaw stance?

1177. Who was the WBC world super-bantamweight champion at the time of the Nishioka v. Kiatisakchokchai contest - Israel Vázquez, Rafael Márquez or Oscar Larios?

1178. True or false: Former British and Commonwealth middleweight champion Johnny Pritchett did not contest a world title during his career?

1179. David Haye, Jhonny González and Orlando Salido were all born in which year – 1979, 1980 or 1981?

1180. The film Somebody Up There Likes Me was based on which former world middleweight champion - Rocky Graziano, Jake LaMotta or Paul Pender?

ROUND 119
NASHIRO REGAINS WBA WORLD SUPER-FLYWEIGHT TITLE

1181. Who was the first holder of the WBC world cruiser weight title - Carlos De León, Marvin Camel or S.T. Gordon?
1182. On 15 September 2008 Nobuo Nashiro regained the WBA super-flyweight title when he defeated defending champion Kohei Kono by which method - 2 round retirement, 6 round stoppage or 12 round points decision?
1183. John Poturaj and Takeo Harada were two of the judges at the Nashiro v. Kono contest, but who was the third - Ricardo Ocasio, Takeshi Shimakawa or Glen Hamada?
1184. In which country did the Nashiro v. Kono contest take place – Thailand, America or Japan?
1185. In which year did Ricky Hatton win the ABA light-welterweight title – 1997, 1998 or 1999?
1186. Which former British heavyweight contender appeared in the comedy film Up the Chastity Belt - Johnny Prescott, Billy Walker or Carl Gizzi?
1187. In how many professional contests did former British, European and Empire welterweight champion Eddie Thomas participate – 47, 48 or 49?
1188. In which weight division was Frankie Jones a British and Empire champion – Flyweight, Bantamweight or Featherweight?
1189. The film Gentleman Jim was based on which former holder of the world heavyweight title - James J. Jeffries, James J. Corbett or James J. Braddock?
1190. True or false: during his professional career British heavyweight contender Johnny Prescott did not box in America?

ROUND 120
RYAN RHODES RETAINS BRITISH LIGHT-MIDDLEWEIGHT CROWN

1191. In which capacity is Miranda Carter involved in professional boxing – Promoter, MC or Boxer?

1192. What is the nationality of trainer Freddie Roach – Canadian, American or Australian?

1193. On 20 September 2008 Ryan Rhodes retained his British light-middleweight title when he defeated challenger Jamie Coyle by which method - 1 round stoppage, 6 round knockout or 12 round points decision?

1194. Where did the Rhodes v. Coyle contest take place – Sheffield, Manchester or Liverpool?

1195. How old was Rhodes at the time of the Coyle contest - 30, 31 or 32?

1196. How old was Coyle at the time of the Rhodes contest – 32, 33 or 34?

1197. In which year did Ryan Rhodes make his professional debut – 1994, 1995 or 1996?

1198. In which year did Jamie Coyle make his professional debut – 2001, 2002 or 2003?

1199. Who was the Commonwealth light-middleweight champion at the time of the Rhodes v. Coyle contest - Bradley Pryce, Ossie Duran or Jamie Moore?

1200. Who was the European light-middleweight champion at the time of the Rhodes v. Coyle contest - Sergei Dzindziruk, Michele Piccirillo or Zaurbek Baysangurov?

ANSWERS

ROUND 1
THE PRIZE-FIGHTING DAYS - 1
1. 1764
2. 6 foot, 2.5 inches
3. The Deaf 'Un
4. American
5. Tom Sayers
6. 18
7. True
8. Bristol
9. True
10. John Camel Heenan

ROUND 2
THE PRIZE-FIGHTING DAYS - 2
11. London
12. William Perry
13. Thomas Winter
14. 1790
15. The Great Gun of Windsor
16. 1858
17. Lawrence
18. The Boston Strong Boy
19. 5 foot, 10.5 inches
20. It was declared a draw after 39 rounds

ROUND 3
WHAT'S MY FIGHTING NAME? - 1
21. Rocky Graziano
22. Joey Maxim
23. Jack Britton
24. Jack (Kid) Berg
25. Jersey Joe Walcott
26. Young Corbert III
27. Kid Gavilan
28. Pancho Villa
29. Kid Williams
30. Philadelphia Jack O'Brien

ROUND 4
WHAT'S MY FIGHTING NAME? - 2
31. Dick Tiger
32. Joe Dundee
33. Midget Wolgast
34. Rocky Marciano
35. Ted Kid Lewis
36. Willie Pep
37. Battling Siki
38. Sugar Ray Robinson
39. Joey Giardello
40. Tony Zale

ROUND 5
NUMBER OF PROFESSIONAL BOUTS - 1
41. 45

42. 122
43. 39
44. 44
45. 37
46. 83
47. 26
48. 35
49. 25
50. 46

ROUND 6
NUMBER OF PROFESSIONAL BOUTS - 2
51. 35
52. 49
53. 27
54. 49
55. 64
56. 201
57. 121
58. 51
59. 46
60. 67

ROUND 7
FIRST DEFEAT - 1
61. Alex Murphy
62. Leonard Del Genio
63. Mike Schreck
64. Lucien Vinez
65. Ray Spackman
66. Doug Jones
67. Harry Leonard
68. Charley Ferguson
69. Andy Escobar
70. Jackie Aldare

ROUND 8
FIRST DEFEAT - 2
71. Max Schmeling
72. Giampaolo Melis
73. Eddie Gill
74. Jim Keery
75. Hilton Smith
76. George Duke
77. Jake LaMotta
78. Singtong Por Tor
79. Albert Finch
80. Ray Davis

ROUND 9
YEAR OF BIRTH - 1
81. 1942
82. 1945
83. 1951
84. 1958

85.	1944
86.	1951
87.	1934
88.	1914
89.	1913
90.	1919

ROUND 10
YEAR OF BIRTH - 2

91.	1951
92.	1942
93.	1935
94.	1926
95.	1950
96.	1966
97.	1946
98.	1948
99.	1939
100.	1913

ROUND 11
DID NOT MEET -1

101.	Scott LeDoux
102.	Herbie Hide
103.	Victor Paul
104.	Johnny Frankham
105.	Emile Griffith
106.	Jim Watt
107.	Herol Graham
108.	Don Waldhelm
109.	Dave Adkins
110.	Aaron Pryor

ROUND 12
DID NOT MEET - 2

111.	Lee Epperson
112.	Charlie Brown
113.	Tom Reddington
114.	Bobby Watts
115.	Rodell Dupree
116.	Richie Sue
117.	Henry Rhiney
118.	Shigeyoshi Ohki
119.	Pedro Carrasco
120.	Johnny Clark

ROUND 13
THE FIRST ROUND - 1

121.	1
122.	2
123.	3
124.	13
125.	13
126.	13
127.	4

128. 5
129. 11
130. 2

ROUND 14
THE FIRST ROUND - 2
131. 5
132. 11
133. 5
134. 13
135. 4
136. 3
137. 3
138. 3
139. 9
140. 1

ROUND 15
FIRST PROFESSIONAL OPPONENT - 1
141. Tunney Hunsaker
142. Barry Price
143. Lupe Guerra
144. Billy Downer
145. Okacha Boubekeur
146. Arley Seifer
147. Sammy Lang
148. Duke Williams
149. Ricky Beard
150. Mike Sullivan

ROUND 16
FIRST PROFESSIONAL OPPONENT - 2
151. John Smith
152. Al Malcolm
153. John Mwaimu
154. Selvin Bell
155. Neil McLaughlin
156. Peter Brown
157. Eddie Godbold
158. Mark Dawson
159. Mario Magriss
160. Hector Mercedes

ROUND 17
FIRST PROFESSIONAL OPPONENT - 3
161. Frank Kary
162. Paul Hanlon
163. Jason Doucet
164. Kid McAuley
165. Tony Booth
166. Clinton Mitchell
167. Michael Johnson
168. Kelly Mays
169. Jerald Lowe
170. Paul Bonson

ROUND 18
FIRST PROFESSIONAL OPPONENT - 4
171. Robert Apodaca
172. Ting Ignacio
173. John Farrell
174. Joaquin Garcia
175. Chris Walsh
176. Stephen Lee
177. John Morton
178. Cam Raeside
179. Dave Proctor
180. Anthony Salerno

ROUND 19
NOT IN THAT COUNTRY - 1
181. Denmark
182. Spain
183. England
184. Mexico
185. Germany
186. Japan
187. England
188. Canada
189. Germany
190. America

ROUND 20
NOT IN THAT COUNTRY - 2
191. Spain
192. England
193. Germany
194. France
195. Belgium
196. England
197. Italy
198. Australia
199. America
200. America

ROUND 21
NATIONALITY - 1
201. American
202. South African
203. English
204. Canadian
205. Puerto Rican
206. American
207. Mexican
208. Mexican
209. American
210. Japanese

ROUND 22
NATIONALITY - 2
211. Hungarian

212. English
213. Mexican
214. Italian
215. Scottish
216. Mexican
217. American
218. American
219. Welsh
220. American

ROUND 23
WHICH WEIGHT? - 1
221. Lightweight
222. Featherweight
223. Welterweight
224. Middleweight
225. Middleweight
226. Lightweight
227. Flyweight
228. Welterweight
229. Light-heavyweight
230. Lightweight

ROUND 24
WHICH WEIGHT? - 2
231. Featherweight
232. Lightweight
233. Middleweight
234. Featherweight
235. Bantamweight
236. Welterweight
237. Light-heavyweight
238. Middleweight
239. Middleweight
240. Featherweight

ROUND 25
NAME THE REFEREE - 1
241. Tim
242. Guido
243. Richie
244. Daniel Van
245. Howard
246. Mark
247. Timo
248. Jeff
249. Ian
250. Wynford

ROUND 26
NAME THE REFEREE - 2
251. Victor
252. Erkki
253. Terry
254. Dave

255. Thabo
256. Richard
257. Paul
258. Mickey
259. Philippe
260. Tony

ROUND 27
TRUE OR FALSE? - 1
261. True
262. False: he was born in 1896
263. True
264. True
265. False: he was born in 1891
266. False: he boxed in the orthodox stance
267. False: he won the world light-heavyweight title
268. True
269. True
270. True

ROUND 28
TRUE OR FALSE? - 2
271. False: he never did
272. True
273. False: he never did
274. False: he won a gold medal at bantamweight
275. True
276. False: he did not box in Denmark
277. True
278. False: he was born in 1961
279. True
280. False: he did not fight at all in America during his professional career

ROUND 29
NAME THE SOUTHPAW - 1
281. Tim Austin
282. Cornelius Boza-Edwards
283. Joe Calzaghe
284. Keith Holmes
285. Tiger Flowers
286. Marvin Hagler
287. Michael Moorer
288. Ruslan Chagaev
289. Steve Molitor
290. Zab Judah

ROUND 30
NAME THE SOUTHPAW - 2
291. Pongsaklek Wonjongkam
292. Alan Minter
293. Stipe Drews
294. Celestino Caballero
295. Ivan Calderon
296. Manny Pacquiao
297. Antonio Tarver

298. Robert Guerrero
299. Jim Watt
300. Juan Urango

ROUND 31
WHO'S THAT LADY - 1?
301. Jane Couch
302. Carol Polis
303. Judith Rollestone
304. The Coal Miner's Daughter
305. Lisa Budd
306. Eva Shain
307. Charlotte Russell
308. Patricia Jarman
309. Tania Follett
310. Scotland

ROUND 32
WHO'S THAT LADY - 2?
311. Jane Couch
312. German
313. Tania Follett
314. True
315. Cathy Brown
316. Diane Lee Fischer
317. Annette Conroy
318. True
319. Holly Holm
320. Jane Couch

ROUND 33
BRITISH CHAMPION IN WHICH WEIGHT DIVISION - 1?
321. Middleweight
322. Light-middleweight
323. Flyweight
324. Light-heavyweight
325. Heavyweight
326. Super-featherweight
327. Heavyweight
328. Super-middleweight
329. Featherweight
330. Middleweight

ROUND 34
BRITISH CHAMPION IN WHICH WEIGHT DIVISION - 2?
331. Super-featherweight
332. Cruiserweight
333. Bantamweight
334. Bantamweight
335. Welterweight
336. Light-welterweight
337. Featherweight
338. Featherweight
339. Light-middleweight
340. Lightweight

ROUND 35
DOUBLE BRITISH CHAMPIONS - 1
341. Middleweight
342. Light-heavyweight
343. Lightweight
344. Middleweight
345. Lightweight
346. Welterweight
347. Flyweight
348. Light-heavyweight
349. Middleweight
350. Bantamweight

ROUND 36
DOUBLE BRITISH CHAMPIONS - 2
351. Welterweight
352. Featherweight
353. Flyweight
354. Featherweight
355. Middleweight
356. Light-heavyweight
357. Lightweight
358. Middleweight
359. Heavyweight
360. Featherweight

ROUND 37
WHAT'S MY NICKNAME? - 1
361. Louisville Lip
362. Homicide Hank
363. Baby Faced Assassin
364. The Dark Destroyer
365. Rapid Fire
366. Hands of Stone
367. Thunder
368. Hitman
369. Hitman
370. The Executioner

ROUND 38
WHAT'S MY NICKNAME? - 2
371. Bronx Bull
372. White Wolf
373. Clones Cyclone
374. Old Mongoose
375. Will o' the Wisp
376. The Quiet Man
377. Lights Out
378. Ghost with a Hammer in his Hand
379. Pottawatomie Giant
380. Man of Steel

ROUND 39
WHOSE NICKNAME - 1?
381. DeMarcus Corley

382. Mike Tyson
383. George Dixon
384. Floyd Mayweather Jr
385. Acelino Freitas
386. Derrick Gainer
387. Joe Frazier
388. Colin McMillan
389. Terry McGovern
390. Érik Morales

ROUND 40
WHOSE NICKNAME - 2?
391. Max Schmeling
392. Joe Louis
393. Kid Chocolate
394. Battling Nelson
395. Gene Tunney
396. Benny Leonard
397. Robert Guerrero
398. Jimmy Wilde
399. Billy Conn
400. Jack (Kid) Berg

ROUND 41
COMMONWEALTH CHAMPIONS - 1
401. Middleweight
402. Light-welterweight
403. Super-middleweight
404. Super-bantamweight
405. Welterweight
406. Featherweight
407. Light-welterweight
408. Light-middleweight
409. Welterweight
410. Super-featherweight

ROUND 42
COMMONWEALTH CHAMPIONS - 2
411. Light-welterweight
412. Light-middleweight
413. Featherweight
414. Middleweight
415. Flyweight
416. Featherweight
417. Light-welterweight
418. Flyweight
419. Light-heavyweight
420. Middleweight

ROUND 43
EUROPEAN CHAMPIONS - 1
421. Bantamweight
422. Flyweight
423. Bantamweight
424. Light-welterweight

425. Heavyweight
426. Featherweight
427. Super-middleweight
428. Light-heavyweight
429. Bantamweight
430. Featherweight

ROUND 44
EUROPEAN CHAMPIONS - 2
431. Welterweight
432. Heavyweight
433. Welterweight
434. Bantamweight
435. Lightweight
436. Bantamweight
437. Middleweight
438. Light-heavyweight
439. Heavyweight
440. Middleweight

ROUND 45
MANAGERS AND PROMOTERS - 1
441. Bob
442. Bruce
443. Rodney
444. Paul
445. Don
446. Joe
447. Lou
448. Jonathan
449. Johnny
450. Barry

ROUND 46
MANAGERS AND PROMOTERS - 2
451. Mick
452. Don
453. Frank
454. Ed
455. Mogens
456. Chris
457. Wilfried
458. Gary
459. John
460. Frank

ROUND 47
PROMOTERS AND MANAGERS - 1
461. Booth
462. González
463. Conroy
464. Hughes
465. Peters
466. Goossen
467. Hobson

468. Duva
469. Sanigar
470. Harding

ROUND 48
PROMOTERS AND MANAGERS - 2
471. Pauly
472. Fernandes
473. Acri
474. Muhammad
475. Cowdell
476. Fondu
477. Finkel
478. Follett
479. Gilmour
480. Ramírez

ROUND 49
THE LAST CONTEST - 1
481. Trevor Berbick
482. Carlos Monzón
483. James Dixon
484. Gene Tunney
485. Harry Jeffra
486. Ralph Chong
487. Alan Minter
488. Brian London
489. Joe Trippe
490. Aurel Toma

ROUND 50
THE LAST CONTEST - 2
491. Ulli Ritter
492. Herschel Joiner
493. R.J. Lewis
494. Terry Downes
495. Davey Abad
496. Sammy Angott
497. Leonard Bennett
498. Alexis Arguello
499. José Legrá
500. Marcel Cerdan

ROUND 51
SUGAR RAY ROBINSON WINS WORLD WELTERWEIGHT TITLE
501. 15 round points decision
502. Eddie Joseph
503. New York
504. 4
505. Clarence Rosen
506. Jack Gardner
507. 15 round points decision
508. 64
509. 8
510. 38

ROUND 52
ROCKY MARCIANO BECOMES NEW WORLD HEAVYWEIGHT CHAMP
511. 25
512. Miami
513. 13
514. Charley Daggert
515. 15 round points decision
516. 9
517. 43
518. 15 round points decision
519. South Africa
520. 6

ROUND 53
HENRY COOPER FAILS IN EUROPEAN HEAVYWEIGHT CHALLENGE
521. 6 round retirement
522. 5
523. Sweden
524. 103
525. Curtis Cokes
526. 15 round points decision
527. Thailand
528. 5 round retirement
529. True
530. Points win for Anderson

ROUND 54
HOWARD WINSTONE WINS VACANT WBC WORLD FEATHERWEIGHT TITLE
531. 1
532. Lewiston
533. 15 round points decision
534. Japan
535. Billy Walker
536. 6
537. 25
538. 9
539. Roland Dakin
540. 65

ROUND 55
KEN BUCHANAN WINS WBA WORLD LIGHTWEIGHT TITLE
541. 10 round points decision
542. 8
543. 15 round points decision
544. Puerto Rico
545. Waldemar Schmidt
546. 15 round points decision
547. 8
548. Australia
549. 7
550. James Brimmell

ROUND 56
CARLOS MONZÓN REIGNS SUPREME
551. 12

552. Solihull
553. 16
554. 13
555. New York
556. John LoBianco
557. 15 round points decision
558. Victor Avendaño
559. Argentina
560. 6

ROUND 57
JOHN CONTEH WINS VACANT WORLD LIGHT-HEAVYWEIGHT TITLE
561. 15 round points decision
562. Glasgow
563. 6
564. 15 round points decision
565. 2
566. 6
567. 15 round points decision
568. England
569. Harry Gibbs
570. 6

ROUND 58
JOHN H. STRACEY WINS WBC WORLD WELTERWEIGHT TITLE
571. 7
572. 4
573. 12
574. Ken Buchanan
575. 6
576. 16
577. 6
578. Mexico
579. Octavio Meyran
580. 47

ROUND 59
MUHAMMAD ALI REMAINS KING OF THE HEAVYWEIGHT DIVISION
581. 15 round points decision
582. West Germany
583. 10
584. Welterweight
585. 13
586. West Germany
587. 10
588. 2
589. 5
590. 10

ROUND 60
JOHN CONTEH RETAINS WBC WORLD LIGHT-HEAVYWEIGHT TITLE
591. Promoter
592. 12
593. Sid Nathan
594. New York

595. 15 round points decision
596. Denmark
597. Harry Gibbs
598. Ghana
599. 9
600. 22

ROUND 61
ALAN MINTER BECOMES EUROPEAN MIDDLEWEIGHT CHAMPION
601. 5
602. Italy
603. A points win for Young
604. 11
605. 1
606. Las Vegas
607. 8
608. Boston
609. A points win for Jones
610. 5

ROUND 62
MAURICE HOPE AND JIM WATT BOTH CAPTURE A WORLD TITLE
611. 8
612. Italy
613. Ray Solis
614. 12
615. Glasgow
616. Arthur Mercante
617. Las Vegas
618. 24
619. 12 round points decision
620. 10

ROUND 63
MARVIN HAGLER WINS UNDISPUTED WORLD MIDDLEWEIGHT TITLE
621. 6
622. Las Vegas
623. 4
624. 15 round points decision
625. America
626. 12 round points decision
627. 10
628. 3
629. England
630. Carlos Berrocal

ROUND 64
SEAN O'GRADY BECOMES NEW WBA WORLD LIGHTWEIGHT KING
631. 54
632. 12
633. Houston
634. 3
635. 10
636. A points win for Mercedes
637. 15 round points decision

638. 12
639. America
640. Richard Greene

ROUND 65
TONY SIBSON FAILS TO WIN WORLD MIDDLEWEIGHT TITLE
641. 3
642. A points win for Márquez
643. 15 round points decision
644. Atlantic City
645. Guy Jutras
646. 6
647. America
648. 15
649. 6
650. John L. Gardner

ROUND 66
A HEAVYWEIGHT CALLED MIKE TYSON LOOKS A FUTURE CHAMP
651. Switzerland
652. America
653. 2
654. 3
655. 4
656. England
657. 12 round points decision
658. 9
659. 12
660. Houston

ROUND 67
HONEYGHAN WINS AGAINST THE ODDS
661. 15 round points decision
662. Atlanta
663. 11
664. 12
665. 6
666. 7
667. America
668. 28
669. 10 round stoppage
670. 10 round points decision

ROUND 68
NIGEL BENN BECOMES NEW COMMONWEALTH MIDDLEWEIGHT CHAMP
671. WBA
672. Australia
673. 7
674. 8
675. 11
676. 7
677. 2
678. Japan
679. 2
680. 10

ROUND 69
CHRIS EUBANK CONTINUES UNDEFEATED RUN
681. 7
682. 12 round points decision
683. England
684. 6
685. 3
686. 4
687. London
688. 18
689. 2
690. 14

ROUND 70
JAMES DOUGLAS DEFEATS MIKE TYSON TO WIN WORLD HEAVYWEIGHT TITLE
691. 10
692. Japan
693. Octavio Meyran
694. 4
695. 10
696. 12 round points decision
697. France
698. 6
699. 14
700. 3

ROUND 71
DAVE McAULEY RETAINS IBF WORLD FLYWEIGHT TITLE
701. 12 round points decision
702. New York
703. 39
704. 5
705. 3
706. 12 round points decision
707. 4
708. 7
709. 18
710. 9

ROUND 72
PAT CLINTON WINS WBO WORLD FLYWEIGHT TITLE
711. 1
712. 8
713. Australia
714. IBF
715. 1
716. 30
717. 12 round points decision
718. Glasgow
719. 20
720. Walter McGowan

ROUND 73
LENNOX LEWIS AND FRANK BRUNO MEET FOR WORLD HEAVYWEIGHT TITLE
721. 4
722. America
723. 21
724. 1
725. 12 round points decision
726. Glasgow
727. 7
728. Cardiff
729. True
730. 11

ROUND 74
PRINCE NASEEM HAMED RETAINS TITLE
731. 5
732. 12
733. WBC
734. 12 round points decision
735. 12 round points decision
736. A draw
737. 1
738. 2
739. 17
740. WBC

ROUND 75
BERNARD HOPKINS RETAINS WORLD IBF MIDDLEWEIGHT TITLE
741. 9
742. Jimmy Revie
743. 12 round points decision
744. 4
745. Alexander Gurov
746. 3
747. Richie Davies
748. 11
749. Atlantic City
750. 10

ROUND 76
JOE CALZAGHE WINS VACANT WBO SUPER-MIDDLEWEIGHT TITLE
751. 6
752. 15
753. European
754. 12 round points decision
755. 23
756. 4
757. America
758. 4
759. WBC
760. 4

ROUND 77
RICKY HATTON REMAINS UNDEFEATED
761. 10

762.   America
763.   Tania Follett
764.   7
765.   Manchester
766.   30
767.   9
768.   6
769.   6
770.   Jerry Quarry

ROUND 78
LEWIS DEFEATS HOLYFIELD IN UNIFICATION CONTEST
771.   5
772.   28
773.   6
774.   9
775.   5
776.   13
777.   12 round points decision
778.   America
779.   37
780.   11

ROUND 79
GLENN CATLEY WINS WBC SUPER-MIDDLEWEIGHT WORLD CROWN
781.   7
782.   50
783.   10
784.   America
785.   True
786.   12
787.   Germany
788.   6
789.   3
790.   5

ROUND 80
JOE CALZAGHE TURNS BACK CHALLENGE OF RICHIE WOODHALL
791.   London
792.   10
793.   Las Vegas
794.   6
795.   11
796.   IBF
797.   10
798.   Sheffield
799.   30
800.   3

ROUND 81
LENNOX LEWIS DEFEATED
801.   12 round points decision
802.   Billy Walker
803.   4
804.   Jason Rowland

805.	5
806.	South Africa
807.	6
808.	5
809.	Dan McAlinden
810.	12 round points decision

ROUND 82
JOE CALZAGHE MAKES ANOTHER SUCCESSFUL DEFENCE OF TITLE

811.	4
812.	Mickey Vann
813.	True
814.	12
815.	4
816.	Denmark
817.	32
818.	4
819.	America
820.	42

ROUND 83
MIKE TYSON FAILS TO REGAIN WORLD HEAVYWEIGHT TITLE

821.	4
822.	10
823.	5
824.	8
825.	Memphis
826.	6
827.	8
828.	5
829.	6
830.	America

ROUND 84
ALEX ARTHUR WINS VACANT BRITISH SUPER-FEATHERWEIGHT TITLE

831.	4
832.	Dave Parris
833.	13
834.	12 round points decision
835.	2
836.	28
837.	9
838.	12 round points decision
839.	4
840.	12 round points decision

ROUND 85
NICKY COOK RETAINS COMMONWEALTH FEATHERWEIGHT TITLE

841.	7
842.	Las Vegas
843.	8
844.	True
845.	America
846.	2
847.	Mark Green

848. 21
849. A points win for Rijker
850. 6

ROUND 86
BERNARD HOPKINS CONTINUES TO RULE THE WORLD OF MIDDLEWEIGHTS
851. 2
852. Cardiff
853. 36
854. 1
855. 2
856. 9
857. 12 round points decision
858. Atlantic City
859. 1
860. 7

ROUND 87
CARL FROCH BECOMES KING OF COMMONWEALTH SUPER-MIDDLEWEIGHTS
861. 12 round points decision
862. Marcus McDonnell
863. 12
864. 4
865. British
866. 12 round points decision
867. 2
868. 2
869. America
870. 2

ROUND 88
MIKKEL KESSLER WINS VACANT WBA WORLD SUPER-MIDDLEWEIGHT TITLE
871. 9
872. 8
873. Las Vegas
874. 18
875. 7
876. Denmark
877. 35
878. 12 round points decision
879. New York
880. America

ROUND 89
RICKY HATTON CAPTURES IBF WORLD LIGHT-WELTERWEIGHT TITLE
881. 12 round points decision
882. America
883. 6
884. Germany
885. 39
886. 11
887. 39
888. 12 round points decision
889. Australia
890. 10

ROUND 90
JERMAIN TAYLOR WINS WORLD MIDDLEWEIGHT TITLES
891. Spain
892. 6
893. 12 round points decision
894. 8 round retirement
895. WBC
896. 5
897. Australia
898. 3
899. True
900. 12 round points decision

ROUND 91
RICKY HATTON WINS WBA WORLD WELTERWEIGHT TITLE
901. 9
902. 12 round points decision
903. 41
904. 8
905. 6
906. 12 round points decision
907. Boston
908. 4
909. 6
910. 12 round points decision

ROUND 92
JUNIOR WITTER WINS VACANT WBC WORLD LIGHT-WELTERWEIGHT CROWN
911. Featherweight
912. Heavyweight
913. 9
914. Carmarthen
915. 12 round points decision
916. 37
917. 10 round points decision
918. 10 round points decision
919. 10
920. 3

ROUND 93
FLOYD MAYWEATHER JR DEFEATS OSCAR DE LA HOYA
921. 12 round points decision
922. Las Vegas
923. 42
924. 6
925. Phil Edwards
926. 12 round points decision
927. 38
928. 12 round points decision
929. Phil Edwards
930. 11

ROUND 94
PAULIE MALIGNAGGI WINS IBF LIGHT-WELTERWEIGHT CROWN
931. 30

932. 12 round points decision
933. 1980
934. True: Jane was defeated by Jaime Clampitt
935. 4
936. America
937. 12 round points decision
938. 12 round points decision
939. Stuttgart
940. Heavyweight

ROUND 95
COLIN LYNES IS NEW EUROPEAN LIGHT-WELTERWEIGHT KING
941. 4
942. 11
943. 8
944. 8
945. Ted Bami
946. Welterweight
947. 12 round points decision
948. Johnny Nelson
949. 12 round points decision
950. Lightweight

ROUND 96
CALZAGHE DEFEATS KESSLER
951. Australian
952. Draw
953. 12 round points decision
954. Mike Ortega
955. 39
956. 44
957. Brian London
958. IBF
959. 1962
960. True

ROUND 97
DAVID HAYE KING OF THE CRUISERWEIGHT DIVISION
961. 7
962. France
963. 4
964. Guido Cavalieri
965. 1
966. Howard Foster
967. 12 round points decision
968. 12 round points decision
969. 10
970. Joe Cortez

ROUND 98
TARVER DEFEATS WOODS TO REGAIN IBF WORLD LIGHT-HEAVYWEIGHT TITLE
971. Las Vegas
972. 12 round points decision
973. Atlantic City
974. 12 round points decision

975. 12 round points decision
976. Super-featherweight
977. 2
978. 12
979. 12 round points decision
980. America

ROUND 99
JOE CALZAGHE DEFEATS BERNARD HOPKINS IN AMERICA
981. 12 round points decision
982. 1
983. Joe Cortez
984. Las Vegas
985. True
986. 12 round points decision
987. 12 round points decision
988. Italy
989. 12 round points decision
990. True

ROUND 100
KESSLER REGAINS WBA WORLD SUPER-MIDDLEWEIGHT CROWN
991. 12 round points decision
992. IBO - Ricky outpointed challenger Juan Lazcano over 12 rounds
993. 7 round stoppage
994. 24
995. 5
996. 12 round stoppage
997. Denmark
998. 3
999. True
1000. 11

ROUND 101
COTTO MEET'S WITH DEFEAT
1001. 12 round points decision
1002. Dave Parris
1003. 1
1004. Terry O'Connor
1005. 10
1006. Jack Reiss
1007. 11
1008. Kenny Bayless
1009. Las Vegas
1010. 32

ROUND 102
ANTHONY MUNDINE DEFEATS CRAZY KIM
1011. Jerry Roth
1012. Mexican
1013. Puerto Rican
1014. Flyweight
1015. 1965
1016. Points win for Lujan
1017. Lightweight

1018. 10 round points decision
1019. Australia
1020. 12 round points decision

ROUND 103
NAITO RETAINS WBA WORLD FLYWEIGHT CROWN
1021. European
1022. 10
1023. Frank Garza
1024. Japan
1025. 12 round points decision
1026. 5
1027. Earl Brown
1028. America
1029. Howard Winston
1030. 1991

ROUND 104
JOSHUA CLOTTEY WINS VACANT IBF WORLD WELTERWEIGHT TITLE
1031. 'Blue Moon'
1032. Silver
1033. WBA
1034. Rocky Graziano
1035. Alan Minter
1036. WBO
1037. 9
1038. Robert Byrd
1039. Las Vegas
1040. Ghanaian

ROUND 105
JAMES DEGALE WINS OLYMPIC GOLD MEDAL
1041. 10 round points decision
1042. Gene Del Branco
1043. Japan
1044. 10
1045. Commonwealth
1046. Canada
1047. Middleweight
1048. Cuban
1049. Marvin Hagler
1050. WBO

ROUND 106
MIJARES RETAINS WORLD WBC AND WBA SUPER-FLYWEIGHT TITLES
1051. 10 round points decision
1052. Germany
1053. 10
1054. Charlie Fitch
1055. Canada
1056. 2
1057. Raúl Caiz Jr
1058. 3
1059. Toby Gibson
1060. Mexico

ROUND 107
TALLEST MAN TO HOLD A VERSION OF THE WORLD HEAVYWEIGHT TITLE
1061. 12 round points decision
1062. Germany
1063. Derek Milham
1064. 7 foot
1065. Billy Walker
1066. 5
1067. WBO
1068. 8
1069. False
1070. Rocky Marciano

ROUND 108
MUNROE RETAINS EUROPEAN SUPER-BANTAMWEIGHT TITLE
1071. 6
1072. Sweden
1073. IBF
1074. 5
1075. WBA
1076. Atlantic City
1077. False
1078. 12 round points decision
1079. Nottingham
1080. 10

ROUND 109
NICKY COOK WINS WBO WORLD SUPER-FEATHERWEIGHT TITLE
1081. Russia
1082. WBC
1083. True: 1999 and 2001
1084. 12 round points decision
1085. Mickey Vann
1086. Featherweight
1087. Manchester
1088. 10 round points decision
1089. True
1090. Super-heavyweight

ROUND 110
AMIR KHAN'S FIRST DEFEAT IN THE PROFESSIONAL RANKS
1091. 1
1092. 19
1093. 18
1094. 21
1095. 25
1096. Colombian
1097. Terry O'Connor
1098. True
1099. John Murray
1100. False: Khan had not boxed at all in America at that time of his professional career

ROUND 111
SMALL WINS TITLE
1101. Jake LaMotta
1102. 1954
1103. 10
1104. Terry O'Connor
1105. London
1106. Ryan Rhodes
1107. 6
1108. Super-heavyweight
1109. Joe Louis
1110. Rubin Carter

ROUND 112
VERNON FORREST REGAINS WBC WORLD LIGHT-MIDDLEWEIGHT CROWN
1111. Super-heavyweight
1112. 11
1113. Tony Weeks
1114. 12 round points decision
1115. 37
1116. The Viper
1117. Vic Drakulich
1118. Las Vegas
1119. True
1120. 1976

ROUND 113
KOTELNIK RETAINS WBA WORLD LIGHT-WELTERWEIGHT CHAMPIONSHIP
1121. Henry Cooper
1122. 12 round points decision
1123. Jack Reiss
1124. Mexican
1125. Venezuelan
1126. 12 round points decision
1127. Ukrainian
1128. Japanese
1129. Stanley Christodoulou
1130. David Barnes

ROUND 114
BRADLEY RETAINS WBC WORLD LIGHT-WELTERWEIGHT TITLE
1131. 12 round points decision
1132. Desert Storm
1133. 23
1134. 25
1135. America
1136. Ajose Olusegun
1137. 5
1138. 1971
1139. 1
1140. Will Smith

ROUND 115
BALOYI RETAINS HIS IBF WORLD SUPER-FEATHERWEIGHT TITLE
1141. 3

1142. 33
1143. Argentinian
1144. South African
1145. True
1146. True
1147. Sparkle Lee
1148. South Africa
1149. 12 round points decision
1150. False: Calzaghe and Chilembe had not fought each other at all in the professional ranks

ROUND 116
JACKIEWICZ WINS EUROPEAN WELTERWEIGHT TITLE
1151. 12 round points decision
1152. Mikael Hook
1153. Paul Williams
1154. False
1155. Kell Brook
1156. Gary Jacobs
1157. 10 round points decision
1058. Steve Grey
1159. Wigan
1160. 2005

ROUND 117
GONZÁLEZ WINS WBA WORLD STRAWWEIGHT TITLE
1161. Murray Sutherland
1162. 12
1163. 103
1164. Herbie Hide
1165. True
1166. 4 round stoppage
1167. 21
1168. 29
1169. Nicaraguan
1170. Japanese

ROUND 118
SAME YEAR OF BIRTH
1171. False
1172. 10
1173. 1977
1174. 12 round points decision
1175. Kenny Bayless
1176. True
1177. Israel Vázquez
1178. True
1179. 1980
1180. Rocky Graziano

ROUND 119
NASHIRO REGAINS WBA WORLD SUPER-FLYWEIGHT TITLE
1181. Marvin Camel
1182. 12 round points decision
1183. Takeshi Shimakawa

1184. Japan
1185. 1997
1186. Billy Walker
1187. 48
1188. Flyweight
1189. James J. Corbett
1190. True

ROUND 120
RYAN RHODES RETAINS BRITISH LIGHT-MIDDLEWEIGHT CROWN
1191. Promoter
1192. American
1193. 12 round points decision
1194. Sheffield
1195. 31
1196. 32
1197. 1995
1198. 2003
1199. Bradley Pryce
1200. Zaurbek Baysangurov

www.apexpublishing.co.uk